THE TRINITY

The Trinity

Eternity

&

Time

Thomas G. Weinandy, OFM, Capuchin

SAPIENTIA PRESS

OF AVE MARIA UNIVERSITY

Sapientia Press
of Ave Maria University
5050 Ave Maria Blvd.
Ave Maria, FL 34142
800-537-5487
Distributed by:
The Catholic University of America Press
c/o HFS
P.O. Box 50370
Baltimore, MD 21211
800-537-5487

Cover Design: Kachergis Book Design
Cover Image: mandritoiu/stock.adobe.com
Printed in the United States of America.
Library of Congress Control Number: 2022934042
ISBN: 978-1-932589-86-3

To

St. Lawrence of Brindisi, OFM, Cap.

Doctor of the Church

With the title Apostolic Doctor

CONTENTS

THE TRINITY

Introduction

Back in the early to mid 1970s, when I was working on my PhD dissertation, on the immutability of God and the Incarnation, I came to realize that the issue of eternity and time and their relationship may be the most vexing, both philosophically and theologically. Over the ensuing years, I have pondered, off and on, what it means for God to be eternal and what is the nature of time. Only if God's eternity is properly conceived and clearly articulated is one able to address the mystery of God's relationship to the created world, wherein there is the flow of time. Likewise, one must also properly conceive and clearly articulate the nature of time, for only then can one address the mystery of creation's relationship to the eternal God. In this book, I wish to address these various interrelated questions with the hope of bringing some new clarity and understanding to this perennial and ongoing philosophical debate and theological discussion.

That said, I first want to state two governing principles that have guided my thought over these many years of contemplating God's eternity, creation's time, and their interrelationship. First, the issues at hand are not problems to be solved; that is, the objective is not to obtain a comprehensive understanding of God's eternity, creation's time, and their interrelationship.[1] As with all divine

1. If one thinks that such a comprehensive understanding is possible, one does not grasp correctly the subject matter that one seeks to address. More so, if one

mysteries, the end for which one studies God's eternity, creation's time, and their relationship is to acquire a proper understanding and clear articulation of what exactly the mystery is. Although it is impossible to comprehend these divine mysteries, it is possible to know what the mysteries are, and in knowing these mysteries, to rejoice, in awe and love, in their intelligible incomprehensibility.

Second, traditionally, God's "eternity" has been examined as one of the divine attributes under the general heading of *De Deo Uno*.[2] While I will somewhat do the same, I will more extensively examine "eternity" from the perspective of God being a trinity of persons—the Father, the Son, and the Holy Spirit, for God as God is never simply the "one" God, but rather eternally a trinity of persons. Thus I believe that the traditional treatment of "eternity" has not been fully adequate. To appreciate the entire mystery of divine eternity, it is necessary to place it within its proper theological and therefore correct metaphysical context, that is, within the "eternal" Trinity. Such a context will influence how the Trinity's relation to creation as creation's author is conceived, and the ensuing relationship between divine eternity and creation's time.[3] Because I will

---

believes that one has obtained a complete understanding of eternity and time, and their relationship, one can be assured that one has fallen into error, and maybe, from a Christian perspective, into heresy.

2. I primarily follow Thomas Aquinas's schema as found in his *Summa Theologica*. Although I substantively agree with Aquinas's arguments and conclusions on the various related issues, I will nonetheless disagree with him on others, and in so doing attempt to clarify and develop his teaching.

3. For another study of eternity from within a Trinitarian perspective, see E. Kim, *Time, Eternity, and the Trinity: A Trinitarian Analogical Understanding of Time and Eternity* (Eugene, OR: Pickwick Publications, 2010).

Kim's treatment significantly differs from my own, both in its content and conclusions. As found in Aquinas, we treat both the classic understanding of eternity and time as well as their relationship. Moreover, unlike myself, he engages extensively with other contemporary authors, such as Karl Bath, Paul Helm, Karl Rahner, and Hans Urs von Balthasar. Most importantly, his novel proposal that

extensively treat the metaphysics of the Trinity as a prolegomenon to examining the nature of eternity, it will take a fair bit of time before we reach eternity!

After completing the examination of the eternal Trinity's relation to time within the context of the divine act of creation, I will then address the new salvific relationship between the Trinity and creation, particularly with human persons, founded upon the Trinity's acts of salvation. These acts specifically entail the Incarnation of the Son of God, his death and resurrection, and the outpouring of the Holy Spirit. To partake of the benefits of these saving acts, one must come to faith in Jesus, as Savior and Lord, be baptized, and then partake of the Eucharist. Within this salvific context, human persons, and creation as a whole, are subsumed into the life of the Trinity, and so the relationship between creation's time and the Trinity's eternity differs in kind, and not simply in degree, from the relation that was first established within the act of creation. Such an understanding, I believe, has never been adequately addressed. I hope, at the least, to make a start.

This fairly short book is divided into two parts. The first examines what it means for the Trinity to possess the attribute of eternity, and then the nature of time within the created order. Following upon these two issues, I address the relationship, founded upon the act of creation, that is established between the eternal Trinity and the created order of time. In the second part of our study, I consider the saving actions of the Trinity within time and the ensuing subsequent relationships that exist between the persons of the Trinity and Christians, particularly as found within the sacraments

---

the eternal persons of the Trinity possess their own singular form of "time" is, as will become evident, contrary to my own understanding of what it means for the Trinity to be eternal. Lastly, he does not consider the relationship between eternity and time in the light of the Trinity's salvific works—Part II of my study.

of baptism and the Eucharist. It is through these sacraments that the faithful on earth, within the context of time, are taken up into the very life of the eternal Trinity and so share in the divine attributes of imperishability and immortality.[4]

With this introduction in mind, we can now proceed to the examination of the Trinity's eternity in relationship to creation's time.[5]

---

4. The topic of the relationship between eternity and time has a long academic history, one that reaches back to the Fathers of the Church and progressing through the Scholastics in the Middle Ages down to the present time. Many authors through the centuries have offered multiple perspectives. Recent philosophers and theologians have admirably contributed a great deal to this ongoing endeavor of adequately addressing the relationship between eternity and time. The contemporary authors that I have found most helpful, though I may not always be in entire agreement with their arguments and conclusions, are the following: David Braine, David Burrell, Harm Goris, Paul Helm, Norman Kretzmann, Brian Shanley, and Eleonore Stump. The reader can find their works, along with the other works that I have consulted, in the list of works consulted at the end of this book.

My primary aim in authoring this book on the Trinity and the relationship between eternity and time is to offer my own philosophical and theological reflections to this centuries-old academic enterprise, some of which I consider original. In the light of this intention, I decided not to interact extensively with the multitude of authors and the various opinions they propose. I felt to do so would clutter the present task and place my thoughts in an endless discussion with the views of so many others. Nonetheless, I will note agreements or criticisms at appropriate points.

5. Before we proceed, I must acknowledge a great deal of debt to Nicholas Lombardo, OP, and Thomas Piolata, OFM, Cap. Nicholas offered many beneficial comments as well as demanding challenges to my arguments and clarity of thought. Thomas likewise provided insightful comments. I am especially grateful for his alerting me, from his own study, to Bonaventure's understanding of the Trinity in relation to eternity and time. This is so much the case that at times Bonaventure's thought becomes a subscript to my own primarily Thomistic thought. This is not to say that either fully agree with all that I propose here.

Part I

CHAPTER ONE

The Trinity

Subsistent-Relations-Fully-in-Act

Introduction

This opening chapter is a prolegomenon to examining the nature of
the Trinitarian attribute of eternity. It first examines the philosophical understanding of the one God, that is, God being *ipsum esse*
(being itself) and so *actus purus* (pure act). Second, this chapter
examines the identities of the persons of the Trinity, the Father,
the Son, and the Holy Spirit as they exist and relate to one another.
I argue that the persons of the Trinity are distinctly identified as
subsistent-relations-fully-in-act. Lastly, I more specifically address
the person of the Holy Spirit as Love-fully-in-Act. Only if the Holy
Spirit and his relationship to the Father and the Son is properly
conceived and articulated, which I hold has not been done within
the theological tradition, will a correct understanding of the entire
Trinity be achieved. This proper understanding directly bears upon
a right interpretation of divine eternity.[1]

1. Since I will significantly modify Aquinas's understanding of the Trinity, one

God as the Pure Act of Being

The nature of God's eternity is founded upon the manner in which God exists. Traditionally, most scholars who wish to uphold God's eternity argue, following Aquinas, that one comes to a knowledge of God's existence by distinguishing his manner of existence from that of creation's manner of existence. While Aquinas famously provides five arguments for God's existence in his *Summa Theologica*, I have found his argument in his early work *De Ente et Essentia* to be the most convincing.[2]

When considering God from natural reason alone, Aquinas argues that the existence of God, "in so far as it is not self-evident to us, can be demonstrated from those of his effects which are known to us."[3] When observing objects, we perceive that they exist, but nothing within their nature demands that they exist, nor can they account for their own existence. Thus, for Aquinas, what a thing is, its nature (*essentia*), is distinct from that it is, its being (*esse*).[4] Because entities do not *necessarily* exist and cannot account for their own existence, "everything whose being is distinct from its nature must have being (*esse*) from another."[5] Since *esse* is required for things to exist, there must be a being whose very nature or essence is "to be," whose nature is simply *ipsum esse*, being itself, and thus

---

can find an excellent exposition of his Trinitarian thought in Gilles Emery's book *Trinity in Aquinas* (Ave Maria, FL: Sapientia Press, 2003). Also, see the classic study of Matthias Joseph Sheeben, *The Mysteries of Christianity* (St. Louis: B. Herder, 1946), 25–148.

2. See *Summa Theologica* I, 2, 3. Hereafter *ST*. All quotations will be taken from the *Summa Theologica*, translated by the Fathers of the English Dominican Province (New York: Benziger Brothers, 1947).

3. *ST* I, 2, 2.

4. See *De Ente et Essentia* 4, 6.

5. *De Ente et Essentia* 4, 7. Translation from Armand Maurer, *On Being and Essence* (Toronto: Pontifical Institute of Mediaeval Studies, 1968). See also *ST* I, 3, 4.

able to give *esse*, existence, so that entities can come to be. Such a being is called "God."[6]

While creatures possess *esse*, and so can perform acts whereby they enact their potential, God, being *esse* itself, possesses no ensuing potential whereby he needs to actualize himself more fully.[7] Unlike creatures, then, who are signified by nouns—rock, tree, man—God is simply signified by the verb "to be," and therefore he is "pure act," the pure perfection of being itself. God, whose nature is the same as his existence, that is, "being itself," is therefore not contained in any genus, for he is singular as to the manner of his existence. God's existence as "pure being" therefore differs in kind from all else that is. Moreover, this does not mean that God is his own genus, for this would imply that God's manner of existence only differs in degree, and not in kind, from all else that exists—as if God and all else that existed are subspecies under the overarching genus of "being." While God brings things into existence, and although there is a hierarchy of beings among creatures, God, as "being itself," is not the apex of this hierarchical order, for he does not exist within the created hierarchical order, and therefore the term "genus" does not apply to him in any manner.[8] For Aquinas, this understanding of God as "pure being" is in accord with and is confirmed by what God revealed to Moses. God revealed to Moses that his proper name is He Who Is, which, for Aquinas, signifies "existence itself."[9]

6. See *ST* I, 3, 4.

7. God does possess positive potential—that is, the ability to do what he alone, as "being itself," is empowered to do—such as to bring things into existence (*ST* I, 25, 1–3).

8. See *ST* I, 3, 5. I emphasize this last point because it pertains to the manner in which God is eternal. If God were the apex of a hierarchical order that included himself and all else that is, then he could not be eternal strictly speaking, for he would be ensconced within the created ontological order that, by nature, includes time.

9. *ST* I, 13, 11. Because God is "being itself," only God can comprehend himself.

Now, although we can know that God is "being itself," we cannot comprehend what it means for God to be "being itself"—it
is beyond our intellectual capability, and thus it is impossible
to imagine what it would be like to be "being itself." Because of
God's incomprehensibility, Aquinas states that "we have no means
for considering how God is, but rather how he is not."[10] Thus, for
Aquinas, since God is "being itself," he is simple in that he is not
composed of parts, such as possessing a body, or matter and form.
Rather, his nature and being are one and the same, for his essence
is simply "to be."[11] As noted above, this means that while creatures
have natures that differ from their existence and which are desig-
nated by "nouns," God, being "being itself," is "pure act." Therefore, while we designate such a being by the noun "God," that noun
signifies the pure act that God is in being the act of pure being.
Thus we must constantly remember that the term "God" denotes
a "verb." For example, we speak of a "man running," whereby the
man is performing the act of running. We never speak of "running"
apart from him who is running—the man. Moreover, we speak of
an existing woman, but we never speak of "existing" apart from
her who is "existing"—the woman. But with God, such is not the
case—God is simply the verb, "to be," the pure act of being itself.[12]

We can know that he is pure being, but we cannot comprehend "being itself" (see
ST I, 12, 7).

10. *ST* I, 3, prologue.

11. See *ST* I, 3, 1–8.

12. Eleonore Stump finds fault with the traditional understanding of Aquinas's
notion that God's nature or essence and his being are one and the same—that what
he is (*quid est*) is being itself (*ipsum esse*). She argues that if God were simply "being itself," he would not be an entity, an *id quod est*—a "that which is." Confirming
Alvin Platinga's conclusion, Stump contends that if God were not an entity, an *id
quod est*, he would not exist. Likewise, if God were not an entity, God would not be
a person with an intellect and will. Moreover, the traditional divine attributes could
then no longer be attributed to God, for there would be no "that-ness" to which

God therefore does not perform acts apart from the pure act that he is; that is, God always, by ontological necessity, acts by the pure act that he himself is.[13]

Following upon his treatment of God's simplicity, Aquinas examines God's perfection, goodness, infinity, immutability, and eternity. Before addressing these issues in chapter 2, I want first to examine the nature of the Trinity, particularly the manner in which it is "being itself," and so "pure act," for only in grasping the manner in which the Trinity exists can we ascertain the manner of its perfection, goodness, infinity, immutability, and eternity.

---

they would apply. Thus, in order to preserve his personal existence, with all that this implies, God must be conceived of as an entity, an *Id quod est*. See E. Stump, "God's Simplicity," in *The Oxford Handbook of Aquinas*, ed. B. Davies and E. Stump (Oxford: Oxford University Press, 2012), 135–46.

Stump obviously holds that God as "being itself" entails a "that-ness" or a "what-ness" that differentiates him as a distinct singular being or entity. While Stump does so in order be able to hold that God is personal and possesses the traditional divine attributes, what she has actually done is ensconced God within the generic order of being, though at its pinnacle. What she fails to grasp is that to be "being itself" entails within it the absolute perfections of "to be," which demands an intellect and a will that are perfectly in act and so a personalism that is fully in act. Moreover, it is precisely because God is the pure act of being that all the divine attributes accrue to him, such as eternity. All else that exists possesses a "that-ness" or a "what-ness" by which entities are differentiated and identified. But God does not need to possess a "that-ness" of "what-ness" in order to differentiate him from other entities and to which can be attributed his singular attributes. Rather, his mere singular manner of being as *ipsum esse* differentiates his manner of existence, one that differs in kind from all else that is and so identifies him as God. See also Eleonore Stump and Norman Kretzmann, "Absolute Simplicity," *Faith and Philosophy: Journal of the Society of Christian Philosophers* 2, no. 4 (1985): 353–82.

13. More will be said of this in due course.

The Trinity as
Subsistent-Relations-Fully-In-Act

The above knowledge, concerning the nature of God's existence, is obtained through the use of reason alone. Through divine revelation, however, we have come to know that the one God is a trinity of persons—the Father, the Son, and the Holy Spirit. Although the knowledge we have obtained concerning the existence of God may be prior, at least as an academic exercise, to what has been divinely revealed, what has been revealed is the ultimate source of what we have learned from reason. Thus while reason may discern that there is one God whose nature is "being itself," the ontological foundation that God's nature is "being itself" is that the one God is the Father, the Son, and the Holy Spirit. The question at hand is: In what manner is the Trinity the metaphysical basis for God being "pure being"—an understanding that can be obtained by reason? If there is no such ontological basis within the Trinity, then what was thought to be obtained by reason would be erroneous.[14]

We must begin by first defining what it means for God the Father to "Father."[15] To be "God the Father" necessitates a divine

---

14. Although what I will now conceive and articulate is founded upon the early church councils, particularly Nicaea (325) and Constantinople (381) as well as the Western tradition as found in Augustine, Aquinas, and to some extent, Bonaventure, I will do so in a manner that I think clarifies and develops this received magisterial and theological tradition. Such a development, as stated in this book's introduction, will bear upon the correct notion of divine eternity.

15. Aquinas states:

Now the divine persons are multiplied by reason of their origin: origin includes the idea of someone that from whom another comes, and of someone that comes from another, and by these two modes a person can be known. Therefore, the person of the Father cannot be known by the fact that he comes from another; but by the fact that he comes from no one; and thus the notion that belongs to him is called *innascibility*. As the source of another, he can be offspring—the begotten Son of God. If God the Father did not beget God the Son, he would not be the Father. Moreover, if the Son is not the perfect image of the Father as the Father's Son, he would not be truly and perfectly God as the Father is God. This would demand that the Father did not give to his Son, within his begetting of his Son, the fullness of his divinity, and therefore the Father would not be truly "Father," for the Son would not be truly "Son." The obvious conclusion to be drawn is that it would then be erroneous to speak of God the Father and God the Son. A divine Trinity would simply not be. The Father, however, in fathering his Son, gives himself completely—that is, all that pertains to his divine fatherhood—to his Son, so that the Son is the Father's perfect image possessing all that pertains to his Father as the Father's Son. Thus, in giving himself completely in begetting his perfect Son, the Father bestows upon his Son the fullness of truth, that is, the whole of what it is for the Father to be Father, and therefore the perfect

---

known in two ways, because of the Son is from him, the Father is known as *paternity*; as the Holy Spirit is from him, he is known by *common spiration*. The Son can be known by *filiation*; and also by another person proceeding from him, the Holy Spirit, and thus he is known in the same way as the Father is known, by *communion spiration*. The Holy Spirt can be known by the fact that he is known by *procession*; but not by the fact that another is from him, as no divine person proceeds from him. (*ST* I, 32, 3)

See also *ST* I, 28, 4; I, 29, 1; I, 36, 2, ad 7; I, 40, 4. Thus the Father is the fount of the plentitude of life and love within the Trinity. Although Aquinas does not employ the above phrase with regards to the Father, it would be in accord with his understanding of the Father's *innascibility*. My good friend and confrere Thomas Piolata, however, informed me that Bonaventure does designate the Father as "the fontal-fullness." See his *Disputed Questions on the Mystery of the Trinity*, q. 8, ad 4 and 7. The translation is taken from *Works of Saint Bonaventure*, vol. 3 (St. Bonaventure, NY: Franciscan Institute, 1979).

Although no person proceeds from the Holy Spirit, I argue that this does not mean that he is not active in accordance with the pure act of Love that he is. That the Spirit does proceed from the Father and the Son is the foundational basis for his own distinct activity within the twofold proceeding.

Son is the Father's perfect Word, the perfect expression of who the Father is. The Son/Word, therefore, is in every respect God as the Father is God.[16]

Therefore God the Father, in begetting his Son, is fatherhood-fully-in-act—the act of giving the entirety of his divine being to his Son so that his begotten Son is the perfect image of himself. The noun "Father" accentuates, then, that "God the Father" is a person, a "who," for it designates the "personal" act that he is, that is, the act of begetting his Son. Yet the personalizing noun "Father" solely expresses "fully-in-act-fathering" or "begetting." In this sense, the term "Father" possesses no "noun-ness," that is, "something" other than being the pure act of begetting. The person of the Father is not a "someone" who performs the act of begetting. Rather, his personal identity, who he is, is simply "the act of begetting" itself. The Father's personal defining characteristic is, then, the act that he is. Such an understanding not only confirms what we have obtained by reason, but it also provides the ontological basis for what reason has discerned—that God, being pure being, is the same as his essence, that is, the pure act of "to be."

Moreover, as the Father is fatherhood-fully-in-act, so the Son must be sonship-fully-in-act. The Son's sonship cannot, therefore, be merely defined by his being "begotten," for that would make him merely a passive recipient of his existence. A mere passive reception of his sonship would negate his being the perfect image of his Father, for his sonship would not be in act as the Father's fatherhood is in act. Such would then equally imply that he is not God as the Father is God and also, therefore, that the Father did not bestow the whole of his divinity upon him. Such would again ne-

16. Aquinas states that "the Father in begetting his Son does not transmit any part of his nature, but communicates his whole nature to him, the distinction only of origin remaining" (ST I, 41, 3). See also I, 33, 1; I, 39, 5; and I, 42, 5.

cessitate that the Father is not actually "Father," for his Son would not truly exist as his perfectly enacted likeness.

Now, since this imaging of his Father completely defines the act that the Son is, this perfect act of imaging not only confirms the Father's fatherhood, but also actively corroborates, and so co-defines, the Father's fatherhood. The Father, as fatherhood-fully-in-act, and the Son, as sonship-fully-in-act, subsist or exist as who they distinctively are in relationship to one another. They are, in accordance with the Augustinian and Thomistic tradition, subsistent relations. But I want to emphasize that they are subsistent-relations-*fully-in-act*, for it is within their fully-in-act relationship that they correlatively define one another. Since both the Father and the Son are fully-in-act, not only does the Father's fully-in-act-fatherhood define his fatherhood and so the Son's sonship, but the Son's fully-in-act-sonship, his being begotten, correlatively defines the Father's fatherhood. Without the Son's fully-in-act-sonship, a sonship he received from his Father, the Father would not be fatherhood-fully-in-act. Thus their perfect perichoretic acts, their intertwining relational acts of fatherhood and sonship, both distinguish them as Father and Son, as well as constitute them as the one God.[17]

17. Because the relationship between the Father and the Son distinguishes them from one another, each possessing a distinct identity, Aquinas states that they "oppose" one another. The Father is Father in opposition to his Son, and the Son is Son in opposition to the Father (see *ST* I, 28, 3 and I, 30, 2). I agree with Aquinas that the relationship between the Father and the Son are oppositional, but I also want to hold that they are complementary, in that the Father complements the Son and the Son complements the Father, and thus their relationship not only distinguishes them from one another, but they also correlatively define one another. Thus their complementary relationships constitute them as the one God.

For example, the relation between a husband and a wife is an oppositional relation. But the relationship that makes the husband and the wife oppositional is the same relationship that makes it complementary. The masculinity of the husband complements the femininity of the wife and so establishes their oneness as husband and wife. Similarly, the oppositional relationship among the Father and

Thus the noun "Son," as with the noun "Father," accentuates that the Son is a person, a "who," for it designates the "personal" act that he is, that is, the act of perfectly imaging his Father, who is equally a "who." Yet in rightly employing the personalizing noun "Son," that noun solely expresses "fully-in-act-sonship." Again, as with the term "Father," the noun "Son" possesses no "noun-ness," that is, "something" other than the pure act of sonship—the pure act of imaging his Father.[18] The person of the Son, therefore, is not a "someone" who possesses the image of his Father, but his personal identity, who he is, is simply the pure act of sonship, his pure act of imaging. Thus, as with the Father, the Son's "nature" or "essence" is the very act that he is—sonship-fully-in-act. In accord with what was stated previously concerning the Father, such an understanding of the Son's sonship not only confirms what we have obtained by reason, but also provides the ontological basis for what reason has discerned—that God, being pure being, is the same as his essence, that is, the pure act of "to be." The significant difference is that we now perceive that the one God, as understood by reason alone, is actually the interrelationship between the Father and the Son.

In the above, the focus has been exclusively on the relationship between the Father and the Son apart from the Holy Spirit. I now want to conceive and articulate anew the procession of the Holy Spirit, and in so doing, I will deviate from the common Latin

Son defines their distinct ontological identities but equally constitutes them as the one God.

18. Nicholas Lombardo also speaks of the Son as "the act of imaging" in a draft article that I have read. I may have been influenced by his phrasing, but in any event, my phrase "the pure act of imaging the Father" is expressive of my own understanding that the Son's sonship is fully-in-act, and therefore his sonship is the act of fully imaging his Father.

tradition, particularly as found in Aquinas. This reconceiving of the procession of the Holy Spirit will help establish a more proper understanding of eternity when it is applied to the Trinity and so is essential to the topic at hand.

Aquinas consistently holds the Aristotelian principle that "nothing can be loved by the will unless it is conceived by the intellect."[19] Within the Trinitarian order, therefore, the Father "first" begets the Son and "then" loves his known Son in the Holy Spirit. I want to argue, however, that inherent within the Father's begetting of his Son is the Father's love of his Son. Authentic "fathering" is a begetting out of love, a love of the one being begotten (though on the human level such is not always the case).[20] The Father's one act of fathering therefore contains both the act of begetting of his Son and the act of spirating or breathing forth of his Spirit of Love. The Spirit of Love proceeds from the Father as the act of love in whom he begets his Son and so the act of love that he bestows upon his Son. Without the procession of the Spirit of Love, the Father would not be the loving Father of his Son, nor would the Son be the beloved Son of his Father.[21] The Father's fatherhood is thus dependent upon his begetting his Son and his spirating of the Spirit, for the Son's sonship is dependent upon his being begotten within the Fa-

19. *ST* I, 27, 3, ad 3.

20. Paul states, "For this reason I bow my knees before the Father, from whom every fatherhood (*patrià*) in heaven and on earth is named" (Eph 3:14–15). All Scripture passages are taken from the Revised Standard Version of the Holy Bible (Catholic ed., 1966).

21. In the above, I am obviously rejecting the Aristotelian principle that only what is first known can then be loved. While what is known to be true is loved, what must also be taken into account is that the will, in love, seeks to know what is yet unknown. Thus love of the truth impels the intellect to seek the truth so that in knowing the truth it can be loved. Thus, as we will see, the Spirit of Love for the Son wells up within the Father within the begetting of his Son such that the Father begets his Son within his love for his Son.

ther's love for him—thus constituting him as the Father's beloved Son. The Son, like the Father, is therefore fully defined as Son by sharing in his Father's Spirit of Love. Moreover, being begotten by the Father in the Father's paternal love for him, the Son, in accord with his being the perfect Father's Son, must therefore love his Father in the same Spirit of Love, the Father's gift of Love, in whom he is begotten. If the Son did not love his Father in the same Spirit of Love in whom he was begotten, he would not be the Father's perfect image, for he would not image his Father's perfect love for him. To be sonship-fully-in-act demands the Spirit-imbued Son's perfect act of filial love for his Father, a Father who begets him in the Spirit's Love. The Son, in loving the Father in the Spirit of Love, again confirms the Father's love-begetting fatherhood, for he reciprocates fully the Father's perfect love for him. In this reciprocal love of the Father for his Son and of the Son for his Father, the Holy Spirit proceeds from the Father and the Son—the reciprocal love of the begetter for the begotten and of the begotten for the begetter. Thus we perceive that both the Father's fatherhood and the Son's sonship consists in the loving paternal and filial acts that they respectively enact in relationship to one another.[22]

Now, as the Father is fatherhood-fully-in-act and as the Son is sonship-fully-in-act, so the Holy Spirit must be Love-fully-in-act, for he proceeds from the fully-in-act Father and the fully-in-act Son. If the Holy Spirit is not fully-in-act Love, it would mean that the Father and the Son are not fully-in-act, for neither would then bestow upon one another the fullness of their divine love. Likewise, if the Holy Spirit is not Love-fully-in-act, he would not be as divine as the Father and the Son are divine, and if such is the

---

22. For Aquinas's arguments that the Holy Spirit proceeds from the Father and the Son, see *ST* I, 36, 2 and I, 36, 4.

case, the Father and Son would not be fully divine either, for it is from them that the Holy Spirit proceeds. Moreover, I again want to emphasize that the Father is fatherhood-fully-in-act only in relation to his Son, and the Son is sonship-fully-in-act only in relation to his Father, and so, within their perichoretic or intertwining relationship, as subsistent-relations-fully-in-act, they corroborate and so correlatively define one another. Likewise, the Holy Spirit is Love-fully-in-act only in relationship to the Father and to the Son. Thus the Holy Spirit is a subsistent-relation-fully-in-act within the perichoretic or intertwining subsistent relationship of the Father and the Son.[23]

Moreover, since the Spirit is Love-fully-in-act, he, in communion with the Father and Son, must enact an act that is in keeping with his identity, for it is impossible for an act not to enact the act that defines it. Now, Aquinas states that "love is the first movement of the will."[24] Although he is speaking in terms of God's act of creation, Aquinas states that God, in his love, wills the good of creatures, of which the primordial good is that of existence itself. Thus God, in love, wills to create, and therefore God's will is the cause of creation—he creates because he loving wills to do so.[25] Moreover, of all that is created "God loves Christ" more than he loves all else, for he willed to give him the greatest good, that is, to be true God; thus Jesus' humanity is the most beloved of the Father because "of the union with the Godhead."[26]

Now, if God lovingly willed to bring creatures into existence, and if he loves the humanity of his Son above all of creation, then how much more does the Father lovingly will to beget his Son, and

23. Aquinas states that "relations result from actions" (see *ST* I, 34, 3, ad 2).
24. *ST* I, 20, 1.
25. See *ST* I, 19, 4.
26. *ST* 1, 20, 4, ad 1 and 2.

in so doing give to him the greatest of all goods—the fullness of his very own divinity.[27] What Aquinas does not take fully into account when addressing the procession of the Holy Spirit is his established understanding of the movement of the will in relationship to love. When first addressing the procession of the Holy Spirit, he states that what "proceeds in God by way of love, does not proceed as begotten, or as son, but proceeds rather as spirit; which name expresses a certain vital movement and impulse, accordingly as anyone is described as moved or impelled by love to perform an action."[28] Aquinas later states that "it is a property of love to move and impel the will of the lover towards the object loved."[29] Although Aquinas does not analogously apply this understanding to the Holy Spirit, I would argue that the Spirit of Love wells up within the Father, proceeds from the Father, as that vital movement or impulse wherein he is moved or impelled to beget his beloved Son—the highest good act the Father could lovingly enact. Thus the Holy Spirit proceeds from the Father as the paternal fully-in-act loving impulse wherein he begets his Son, and he proceeds from the Son as the fully-in-act loving impulse wherein the begotten Son loves his begetting Father.[30]

27. Importantly, in willing to beget his Son in the Love of the Spirit, he equally, though freely, wills all that comes to be, for the Son, as the Word, contains the fullness of Father's divine knowledge. For Aquinas, Word implies relation to creatures. "For God by knowing himself, knows every creature." "Because God by one act understands himself and all things, his one only Word is expressive not only of the Father, but of all creatures" (*ST* I, 34, 3). Moreover, "now as God by one act understands all things in his essence, so by one act he wills all things in his goodness" (*ST* I, 19, 5). What the Father knows in his Word, he lovingly wills in the Spirit to create.

28. *ST* I, 27, 4.

29. *ST* I, 36, 1.

30. Similarly, Aquinas states that "love has the nature of a first gift, through which other gifts are given. So, since the Holy Spirit proceeds as love as stated above (I, 27, 4 and I, 37, 1), he proceeds as the first gift" (*ST* I, 38, 2). Thus, as I pro-

What act, then, does the fully-enacted-Love that is the Spirit enact in relation to the Father and the Son? Within the Spirit's proceeding from the Father and the Son, as they are moved to love one another, the Spirit of Love corroborates and so co-relatively defines the Father as the loving Father of his Son and corroborates and so co-relatively defines the Son as the loving Son of the Father. Proceeding from the Father and the Son within the act of the Father begetting his Son, the Holy Spirit enacts the act wherein the Father loves his begotten Son and the Son loves his begetting Father. The Holy Spirit's identity, as the Love of the Father for his Son and the Love of the Son for his Father, is, then, constituted not only by his procession from them, but also in his corroborative act of bringing their distinct identities as Father and Son to the perfection of their forms, that is, the Father being truly the loving Father of his Son and the Son being truly the loving Son of his Father.[31]

---

pose, in the begetting of his Son in the Love of the Spirit, the Father gives to his Son the gift of Love wherein the Son reciprocates with the gift of Love for his Father.

31. Aquinas, in reference to the Word and Holy Spirit, states, "For as when a thing is understood by anyone, there results in the one who understands a conception of the object understood, which conception we call word, so when anyone loves an object, a certain impression results, so to speak, of the thing loved in the lover; by reason of which the object loved is said to be in the lover" (*ST* I, 37, 1). Thus the Father, Son, and Holy Spirit are perichoretic subsistent-relations-fully-in-act, for they are who they are within their mutual relational abiding in one another, thus constituting themselves as the one God.

Because the Holy Spirit is the mutual love of the Father and the Son, Aquinas also concludes, "The Holy Spirit is said to be the bond of the Father and Son, in as much as he is Love; because since the Father love himself and his Son with one Love and conversely, as that of lover to the beloved" (*ST* I, 37, 1, ad 3). Again, I would accentuate that the Holy Spirit is such a bond of Love precisely because he corroborates and so co-relatively defines the Father to be the loving Father of his Son, as well as the Son to be the loving Son of his Father.

In the light of the above, Thomas Piolata again reminded me that, unlike Aquinas, Bonaventure treated the divine attributes within the context of the Trinity, specifically in his *Disputed Questions on the Mystery of the Trinity*. He recently

Thus the Father, the Son, and the Holy Spirit are all equally subsistent-relations-*fully-in-act*, for it is within their fully-in-act relationships that they, founded upon the Father's fatherhood, correlatively define one another. If their identities as Father, Son, and Holy Spirit were not founded upon their mutual constituted interrelationships, none of them would be who they are, and so, once again, the Trinity would dissolve. Thus their perfect perichoretic acts, their intertwining relational acts of fatherhood, sonship, and love, both distinguish them as Father, Son, and Holy Spirit as well as constitute them as the one God. The Trinity is therefore the eter-

---

completed his Licentiate in Theology at the Gregorian University in Rome, where he wrote his thesis on the role of the Holy Spirit in Bonaventure's Trinitarian thought, "*Unitas Caritatis*: A Reading of Bonaventure's *Quaestiones Disputatae de Mysterio Trinitatis* (With a Focus on the Spirit)." I am grateful to him for sharing with me his thesis. The following summary remarks are gleaned from his excellent study of Bonaventure.

In his *Disputed Questions on the Mystery of the Trinity*, Bonaventure speaks of the unity of the Trinity as a *unitas caritatis*.

> Again, that unity is more perfect in which, together with the unity of nature, there remains the unity of love (*unitas caritatis*). But "love tends toward the other" (Gregory, *I Homil. In Evange.*, homily, 17, n. 1). Therefore, it includes the distinction of the lover and the beloved. Therefore, if the most perfect unity exists in God, it is necessary that he possess an intrinsic plurality for he has nothing outside himself that is supremely loveable (*Disputed Questions*, 2, 2, fund. 9). The translation is taken from *Works of Saint Bonaventure*, III (St. Bonaventure, NY: The Franciscan Institute, 1979).

Thus the Father and the Son find their complete perichoretic unity, their mutual metaphysical bonding, within the love of the Holy Spirit. Although Bonaventure does not speak, as I do, of the Father begetting his Son in the Love of the Spirit, he does hold that, since the Spirit is the unity of charity, he completes, brings to fullness of form, the Father's fatherhood and the Son's sonship, that is, their mutual love for one another. The Father begets his Son so that together they may love one another in the Spirit of Love and so become one. Love initiates the Father's begetting of the Son, and Love terminates in their mutual love for one another. As Piolata summarily states, "The *unitas caritatis* is the *ultimum* of the *ordo trinitatis*. Love completes the order; order is for love."

nal, non-sequential, symmetrical perichoretic fully-in-act relations
of the fully-in-act Father, the fully-in-act Son, and the fully-in-act
Holy Spirit, and therefore correlative acts whereby they coinhere in
one another as the one Triune God.

Again, in keeping with what was discerned concerning the
Father's fatherhood and the Son's sonship, the nominative name
"Holy Spirit" accentuates that the Holy Spirit is a person, a "who,"
for he enacts, in communion with the Father and the Son, the personal act wherein the Father and the Son love one another.[32] Yet in
rightly employing the personal name "Holy Spirit," the Holy Spirit
possesses no "noun-ness," that is, "something" other than being the
pure act of Love—the pure act of Love between the Father and the
Son. The Holy Spirit is therefore not a "someone" who possesses
Love, but rather his personal identity is the pure act of Love that
he is.[33] As with the Father and the Son, the Holy Spirit's "nature"
or "essence" is the very act that he is—Love-fully-in-act. Moreover,
in accord with what was stated previously concerning the Father

32. Because the Holy Spirit is the perfect pure act of self-giving Love that the
Father and Son bestow upon one another, the Holy Spirit does not have a proper
name as do the Father and the Son. For Aquinas, the name "Holy Spirit" is employed because it is found in Scripture. Such a scriptural name is appropriate, for it
expresses what is common to the Father and the Son; that is, both the Father and
the Son are "spirit," and both are "holy." See Aquinas, *ST* I, 27, 4, ad 3; I, 36, 1; I, 37,
1 and 2; and I, 38, 1 and 2.

33. As the pure act of Love, the Holy Spirit, as seen above, perfects the "names"
of the Father and the Son, for the Spirit is the act, the impulse, of love that moves
the Father to beget his Son within his paternal love for his Son, and equally
moves the Son's reciprocal filial love for his begetting Father. The Holy Spirit proceeds, therefore, from the Father and the Son as the unifying pure act of love that
perfects their paternal and filial relationship. Moreover, because the Holy Spirit
does not have a proper name that personally identifies him, since he is the pure
act of love, significantly, he ontologically validates perfectly that the Father and the
Son, for though they rightly possess "noun" names, possess no "noun-ness." They
too are, as is the Holy Spirit, simply "subsistent-relations-*fully-in-act*."

and the Son, such an understanding not only confirms what we
have obtained by reason, but it also provides the ontological basis
for what reason has discerned—that God, being pure being, is the
same as his essence, that is, the pure act of "to be." The significant
difference is that we now perceive more fully who the one God is
as understood by reason alone. The one God is the perichoretic
interrelationship of the Father, the Son, and the Holy Spirit, each of
whom, as befitting their distinct identities, is a subsistent relation-
fully-in-act.[34]

34. Aquinas states that as God's existence was seen to be pure act and so his
existence is the same as his nature or essence, so the persons of the Trinity, since
they are subsistent relations, are the same as their essence (see *ST* I, 39, 1 and 2).
I would stress that it is because the persons of the Trinity are subsistent-relations-
fully-in-act that "who" they are (the three persons) and "what" they are (the one
God) are one and the same. Nonetheless, in acknowledging that persons of the
Trinity are the same as their essence, Aquinas recognizes that what was obtained
through reason, that God is pure being and so his essence is simply "to be," finds its
full and only true metaphysical foundation within the Trinity itself. Therefore all of
the divine attributes that were discussed when treating our knowledge of God by
way of reason alone, including "eternity," also find their authentic and true divine
ontological source within the Trinity.

Before we proceed, I must address the history of my thought concerning the
procession of the Holy Spirit, for it has developed and been revised over time. My
present understanding of the procession of the Holy Spirit is fundamentally in
accord with what I first articulated in my *Father's Spirit of Sonship: Reconceiving
the Trinity* (Edinburgh: T&T Clark: 1995). In this volume, I addressed two issues
that I thought undermined the personhood of the Holy Spirit. Although I agreed
that the Holy Spirit proceeds from the Father and the Son, as found within the
Western theological tradition, particularly within Augustine and Aquinas, I argued
that the Holy Spirit remained passive; that is, he was seen as the love shared by the
Father and the Son. Because the Holy Spirit was not portrayed as an active agent,
it was difficult to uphold that the Spirit is a person, a "who," along with the Father
and the Son. Moreover, Aquinas, following Aristotle's principle that one can only
love what is first known, argues that the Father first begets his Son, and then, in
knowing his Son, comes to love his Son through the Holy Spirit—the Spirit of
love. Thus Aquinas states that there is a certain order. "For the procession of love
occurs in due order as regards the procession of the Word; since nothing can be

loved by the will unless it is conceived in the intellect" (*ST* I, 27, 3, ad 3). There is, then, within the Trinity a "sequentialism" that undermines the truth that Trinity is the perichoretic interrelationship of the Father, the Son, and the Holy Spirit as subsistent-relations-fully-in-act, relationships that constitute them as the one God. Moreover, as we will see, this sequentialism undermines a proper understanding of "eternity" when applied to the Trinity's manner of being.

In order to address these two issues, as seen above, I proposed that the Father spirates or breathes forth his Spirit in the very act of begetting his Son, for the Spirit of Love rises up from within the Father so as the impulse that moves him to beget his Son within his paternal love for his Son. As Aquinas himself states, "We must needs assert that in God there is love; because love is the first movement of the will and of every appetitive faculty" (*ST* I, 20, 1). (As noted above, Aquinas seems to overlook this point when treating of the Holy Spirit directly.) The love that is in the Father is the Holy Spirit, and it is the Spirit of Love that moves the Father within the act of begetting his beloved Son and proceeds to move the Son to love his beloved Father. Such an understanding abandons any notion of sequentialism, for the Father's act of begetting and his act of spiriting, while distinct acts, are enacted together. Moreover, as seen above, the act that is the Spirit is the act of love that brings the Father and Son to their complete form—that of being the loving Father of the Son and the loving Son of the Father. Thus the Holy Spirit is, along with the Father and the Son, a divine person, a "who," for he performs an act in keeping with the pure act that he is—the act of Love itself.

My newly proposed understanding of the procession of the Holy Spirit as found in my book *The Father' Spirit of Sonship* has provoked criticism. See particularly M. Levering, *Engaging the Doctrine of the Holy Spirit: Love and Gift in the Trinity and the Church* (Grand Rapids, MI: Baker Academic, 2016). In the light of this criticism, I now hold that three notions I offered in my book are erroneous. The first is that I spoke of the Father as begetting his Son "by" the Holy Spirit and not simply "in" the Holy Spirit. The term "by" gives the impression that the Father is employing the Holy Spirit as an agent along with himself in begetting his Son. Only the Father is the principle of the Son's existence—he is the only begetter. (Aquinas does defend the use of the term "by," however, in that the Father and the Son love each other "by" the Holy Spirit; see *ST* I, 37, 2.) Although the Spirit is not a principle of the Son's existence, a "begetter," he is the impulse of love within the Father, wherein the Father is moved to beget his beloved Son. Second, I also reject my previous proposal of a *Spirituque*, that is, that the Son is begotten by the Father *and* the Spirit. Such a notion equally implies that the Spirit is a principle, along with the Father, whereby the Son is begotten. Third, I also made some ambiguous statements that in hindsight could easily be misconstrued. In speaking of the relationships between the persons of the Trinity, I spoke of the Holy Spirit as the one who "persons" or "conforms" the Father, and the Son in that the Spirit "makes the Father to be the Father of the Son and makes the Son to be the Son of the Father" (*The Father's Spirit of Sonship*, 72 and 79). Once again, this appears to make the Spirit a principal agent of the Father being the Father and of the Son being the Son. What I was attempting to express, as I have now articulated above, is the fact that the Father would not be truly the person of the Father, and the Son would not be truly the person of the Son, if they did not love one another in the Love that is the Holy Spirit. The Holy Spirit is presently seen as the Love that moves the Father to beget his Son, and so the Father begets his Son in the Love that is the Spirit, and in so doing, the Love that is the Spirit moves the Son to love his Father. The Spirit, then, is not the originate principle of either or both. Rather, the Spirit, who proceeds from both, actively unites them as Lovers in the Beloveds, for in the Love that he is, they abide lovingly in one another, and he co-inheres in them as their abiding Love. For Aquinas, the Holy Spirit is "the unitive love" of the Father and the Son" (*ST* I, 36, 4, ad 1). Ultimately, as expressed above, the point I want to make is that none of the divine persons subsist as who they are apart from their fully-in-act perichoretic relationships. They are subsistent relations fully-in-act. To deprive any one of the divine persons his singular defining relational act(s) is to divest all of the persons of their singular defining relational act(s), and so rob the Trinity of its existence. Thus, as stated above, the persons of the Trinity, in a manner appropriate to each, co-relatively define one another.

For a fuller revised understanding of the procession of the Holy Spirit, see my forthcoming chapter "The Trinity: The Father's Spirit of Sonship—Further Considerations on Reconceiving the Trinity," in *Engaging Catholic Doctrine: Essays in Honor of Matthew Levering*, edited by Robert Barron, Scott W. Hahn, and James R. A. Merrick (Steubenville, OH: Emmaus Academic, forthcoming).

CHAPTER TWO

The Trinity's Eternity

Introduction

Having considered the nature of God as *ipsum esse* and *actus purus*, and the persons of the Trinity as subsistent-relations-fully-in-act, we are now able to examine the attribute of eternity as it pertains to the Trinity. We will first do so by surveying the divine attributes of simplicity, perfection, goodness, and immutability, for they determine the manner in which the Trinity is eternal. Second, we will turn our full attention to the attribute of eternity itself.

The Trinity: Simplicity, Perfection, Goodness, and Immutability

In order to discern the manner in which the Trinity is said to be eternal, I follow the format as found in Aquinas's *Summa Theologica*, where he addresses the divine attributes that pertain to God. Although Aquinas considers these attributes within the context of what reason alone can know concerning God, I treat them in their more proper metaphysical context, that is, as they pertain to the Trinity, for the one God *only* exists as a Trinity of divine persons.

As we saw, because God's essence and existence are the same—that is, the pure act of being—God is utterly simple. He is not composed of parts.[1] Similarly, as we also saw, the persons of the Trinity, as subsistent-relations-fully-in-act, are their own essence. Although their relationships distinguish them from one another, the same relationships constitute them as the one God. Thus the Trinity is absolutely simple, for it is not composed of parts.[2] Moreover, for Aquinas, "A thing is perfect in proportion to its state of actuality," and since God is the pure act of being, God is perfect.[3] Because God is perfection itself, and thus the source all perfections, he is the source of all that exists. Likewise, goodness is founded, again, upon one's state of actually, for the greatest good is to exist. Since God is existence itself, he is goodness itself, and so again the source of all goodness, for he is the source of all that is.[4]

Now, in begetting his Son in the love of the Spirit, the Father is fatherhood-fully-in-act, and so he is the perfection of fatherhood. The Father is the perfect in-act plentitude of life (being) and love. The Son, in being begotten within the Love of the Spirit, is the Father's perfect enacted image, and so he is sonship-fully-in-act, for he is both the in-act likeness of his Father and, in so being, perfectly loves the Father in the same Spirit of Love in which he is begotten. Equally, the Holy Spirit, as Love-fully-in-act, proceeds from the Father and the Son as the one who perfects the Father's fatherhood and the Son's sonship. Thus the persons of the Trinity, founded upon the Father's fatherhood, are perfect, for they each, in accordance with who they distinctively are, possess the fullness of

---

1. See *ST* I, 3, 1–8.

2. See *ST* I, 39, 1–2. On the divine simplicity of the Trinity, see Thomas Joseph White, "Nicene Orthodoxy and Trinitarian Simplicity," *American Catholic Philosophical Quarterly* 90, no. 4 (2016): 727–50; and "Divine Simplicity and the Holy Trinity," *International Journal of Systematic Theology* 18, no. 1 (2016): 66–93.

3. *ST* I, 4, 1.

4. See *ST* I, 5 and 6.

divine life or actuality, and so the full perfection of goodness. Being goodness itself, the persons of the Trinity also love one another perfectly, for perfect love is enacted in loving the perfect good, and the persons of the Trinity are goodness itself, and so the Trinitarian perfection of goodness elicits a perfect Trinitarian act of love. Having considered God's perfect goodness as contained within his being the pure act of being, Aquinas addresses God's immutability, which in turn leads to the nature of God's eternity.

Since he is pure act, Aquinas obviously concludes that God is immutable. There is no potency within God for him to enact that which would make him more actual, for he is the perfect plentitude of being itself.[5] Thus for God to be unchanging does not mean that he is static, lifeless, or inactive. Rather, because God is being itself, he is pure act and thus exists in manner that differs in kind, and not in degree, from all else that exists, for all else that exists undergoes change wherein it enacts its potential or is changed by something other than itself.[6] Thus God is that which nothing greater can be conceived, for the greatest conceivable being is one who is the plentitude of unchangeable being. While God's immutable essence as being itself can be discerned from reason alone, such unchangeability is ontologically founded upon the Trinity. As I have emphasized throughout, the Father is fatherhood-fully-in-act, both in his act of begetting his Son and in his act of loving his Son in his spirating of the Spirit of Love, and therefore no further paternal act could possibly further enact his fatherhood. The Father's beloved begotten Son is sonship-fully-in-act, for not only does he possess the fully-enacted-divinity of his Father, but he also reciprocally loves the Father in the fully-enacted-Love of the Spirit in whom he was begot-

5. See *ST* 1, 9, 1 and 2.
6. William E. Mann argues that God's immutability is founded upon his simplicity. See "Simplicity and Immutability of God," in *The Concept of God*, ed. Thomas V. Morris (Oxford: Oxford University Press, 1987), 253–67.

ten. Therefore no additional filial act could possibly further enact his sonship. The Holy Spirit is Love-fully-in-act, for he is the fully-enacted-love of the Father for the Son and the fully-enacted-love of the Son for his Father; and as the pure act of Love, the Spirit perfects the Father's fatherhood and the Son's sonship. Therefore no additional loving act could possibly further enhance the pure act of Love that the Spirit is. The Father, the Son, and the Holy Spirit are immutable, for they are perichoretic-subsistent-relations-fully-in-act, and no further additional acts could possibly contribute to their being who they perfectly are in relation to one another. Thus, in being immutable, the Father, the Son, and the Holy Spirit, far from being static, lifeless, and inert, are the plentitude of fully enacted life and love. No being can be conceived that is more in act than the Trinity.

The Trinity: Eternity

We finally arrive at the topic of eternity! We have done so only because all of the metaphysical pieces concerning our knowledge of God obtained through the use of reason and concerning our knowledge of the Trinity as obtained through revelation are now in place. Given all of the above, we are able to conceive properly and articulate clearly the meaning of eternity as it applies to the manner of the Trinity's existence.

Regarding eternity, Aquinas states:

> The idea of eternity follows immutability, as the idea of time follows movement. Hence, as God is properly immutable, it supremely belongs to him to be eternal. Nor is he eternal only; but he is his own eternity; whereas, no other being is its own duration, as no other being is its own being. Now, God is his own uniform being; and hence, as he is his own essence, so he is his own eternity.[7]

7. *ST* I, 10, 2.

For Aquinas, because God is the pure act of being, he is unchangeable, and therefore he can be said to be eternal. However, he is not simply eternal, but he is his own eternity in that he is "eternity" itself, for his very nature is simply the unchanging pure act of being itself. Thus God is his own "duration," in that he never ceases to be the pure act of being that he is, which constitutes his eternity.[8] Therefore "eternity" can only be properly applied to the Trinity, since only the Trinity exists as the one God. Thus, because the persons of the Trinity are the immutable, fully perfect, perichoretic relationships that constitute their being subsistent-relations-fully-in-act, the term "eternity" is properly predicated on them. Similar to Aquinas's understanding, they are not only "eternal" but also their own "eternity," for the very manner in which they immutably exist as subsistent-relations-fully-in-act, their very nature, contains within it the notion of "eternity." Timelessness defines their manner of being, for their manner of being constitutes what the term "eternal" means. Without the Trinity, there would be no being to which "eternity" could properly apply.

The Trinity therefore has no "past," for there was no "before" that was prior to their being who they are, and therefore there is no "past" wherein they were not who they are. Likewise, the Trinity possesses no "future," for there is no act that would further constitute who they are as perichoretic-subsistent-relations-fully-in-act. Their fully-in-act relationships perfectly constitute them as fatherhood-fully-in-act, sonship-fully-in-act, and Love-fully-in-act. Thus when the term "eternity" is applied to the manner in which the Trinity exists, it designates a denial that the Trinity possesses a "past" and

---

8. While Aquinas speaks of God's "duration," in the sense of "always" being who he is, I am not happy with this notion of "duration" even though it may be given a proper understanding when applied to God. The reason for my displeasure is that the notion of "duration" is inherently a "time" concept, and no time concept can ultimately be applied to God. I will address this issue shortly.

a "future." The term "eternity" primarily predicates a negative judgment so as to confirm a right understanding of the nature of the Trinity's existence. Such a negative judgment is founded upon the positive manner in which the Trinity does exist—the fully actualized personhood of Father, the Son, and the Holy Spirit.

The question that now arises is whether the Trinity possesses a "present." It may appear that the persons of the Trinity do possess a "present," for they "eternally" *are* who they are. This eternal manner of "being," which constitutes who they are, seems to imply an eternal "present," an eternal "now," for the very verb "to be" (*esse*) appears to manifest or represent a "present." To address this issue, we must examine Aquinas's teaching on divine eternity more closely.

As was common among the Scholastics, Aquinas first argues that Boethius's definition of eternity is suitable. Boethius states, "Eternity is the simultaneous [at once] complete and perfect possession of interminable [unending] life" (*aeternitas est interminabilis vitae tota simul et perfecta possessio*).[9] Aquinas argues, "Thus, eternity is known from two sources: first, because what is eternal is interminable—that is, has no beginning and no end (that is, no term either way); secondly, because eternity has no succession being simultaneously whole."[10] What is eternal, then, always is, and it always is because it does not change, but rather possesses, all at once or simultaneously, the whole of life. In this light, we can turn to Aquinas's next question: "Whether God is Eternal?"

As we already saw, Aquinas holds that God's eternity follows upon his immutability, the pure act of being itself, and thus eternity is contained within the very definition of who he is as pure act. Now, in replying to Boethius's further statement that "the now that

9. *ST* I, 10, 1, obj. 1.
10. *ST* I, 10, 1. See also I, 10, 4.

stands still makes eternity" (*nunc stans facit aeternitatem*), Aquinas
argues that this "now that stands still is said to make eternity according to our apprehension." Because we understand the flow of
time, we speak of a "*now*" within that flow. In doing so, we apprehend eternity as "the standing still *now*," that is, a "now" that has
no movement—a movement from past to present.[11] The question
returns: Does this eternal "standing still now" contain within it an
eternal "present?"[12] Or does "according to our apprehension" mean
that there is actually no "now," no eternal "present," in God, but
rather that we attribute to him such a permanent "now," an eternal
"present," so as to accentuate, unlike created beings who experience the flow of time, God's eternal timelessness? I find it difficult
to judge which of the two positions Aquinas actually holds, yet
I would think that he subscribes to the position that there is no
"now," no "present," that pertains to God's eternity. Nonetheless,
according to our way of thinking, our apprehension, we ascribe
to God an eternal "standing still now," since we exist in time, and
the ascribing of a "standing still now" assists us in understanding
what it means for God to be eternal. As I will argue shortly, to
hold that there is a "now" in God, a "present," negates a proper understanding of eternity, for it undermines God's utter timelessness.
The problem is that the commonly held opinion, especially among
non-academics, is that there is an eternal "now" in God—that there
is a "standing still" permanent "present." The reason for this is that

11. *ST* I, 10, 2, ad 1. See also I, 10, 4, ad 2.

12. The revered interpreter of Thomas, R. Garrigou-Lagrange, when treating
this same first reply, also speaks of the divine "standing still *now*" in relation to our
apprehension. *The One God: A Commentary on the First Part of St. Thomas's Theological Summa* (St. Louis: B. Herder, 1943), 283. Likewise, Matthias Joseph Scheeben addresses this same issue in his *Handbook of Catholic Dogmatics, Book Two:
Doctrine about God, or Theology in the Narrower Sense* (Steubenville, OH: Emmaus
Academic, 2021), 135–36.

if God does not experience an eternal "present," it would seem that he would not experience himself as one who possesses "the simultaneous [at once] complete perfection of interminable [unending] life." Moreover, if he does not experience a present, God would not be aware of creation's and particularly our "present," and so creation's or our past and future.

In the above exposition of Boethius's definition of eternity, there is both a conceptional and a terminological issue. While "interminable" (*interminabilis*) denies of God a "beginning" and an "end," and so God has no past or future, and while "simultaneous whole" (*tota simul*) predicates the all-at-once unchanging perfection of the fullness of life, both concepts carry with them "time-ness," even if the "moment" is the simultaneous perfection of unending life. Thus Boethius's definition unfortunately contains within it an eternal "present," an eternal "now," wherein God eternally exists. Aquinas attempts to eliminate such "time-ness," but his attempt to do so results, as seen above, in some ambiguity. He continues to speak of eternity as a "standing still now," and that "now" is a holdover from Boethius's definition. In the end, Aquinas would have been wise to have provided his own definition of eternity, which I am confident would have been more accurate than Boethius's.

I now want to argue that clarity can only be achieved when the concept of eternity is placed within its more proper metaphysical context—that of the one God being a trinity of persons. As numerously stated, at this point ad nauseam, all of the persons of the Trinity are perichoretic-subsistent-relations-fully-in-act. Such perichoretic relations not only constitute their singular identities, but they also constitute their divine oneness. Because their singular subsistent relations are fully-in-act, they are utterly timeless. They simply are who they are as fully enacted acts in relation to one another. There is neither simultaneity nor all-at-once-ness about these relational fully enacted acts, for the very manner of the fully-in-act acts precludes any timely notion of simultaneity or at-once-ness. Moreover, while they possess the fullness of life owing to their being relations-fully-in-act, their fully-in-act life is not interminable insofar as interminability entails duration. Yet, properly conceived, fully enacted acts entail no duration. As with "a standing still now," we may apprehend eternity as an interminable duration, but the persons of the Trinity themselves simply are timeless perichoretic-fully-in-act relations, and so they are metaphysically devoid of an epistemological or self-conscious experience of "duration"—they timelessly are who they are as the one God. Thus eternity, as found within the Trinity, denotes a timelessness, but such an absence of time is founded upon the fully-in-act-relational-acts that they are—the fullness of life and love that is founded upon the Father's fully enacted fatherhood, a fatherhood that comprises, and so enacts, both the Son's fully enacted sonship and the Spirit's fully enacted Love.

Moreover, as I have consistently stressed, while the Father's spirating of the Spirit of Love is a distinct act, such spiration is enacted within his act of begetting his Son, and so there is no sequence. Such sequential acts would necessitate, or at least logically imply, a "time" factor within the Trinity.[13] The persons of the Trinity would

13. Aquinas states that the persons of the Trinity are eternal:

As the begetting of the Son is coeternal with the begetter (and hence the Father does not exist before begetting the Son), so the procession of the Holy Spirit is coeternal with his principle. Hence the Son was not begotten before the Holy Spirit proceeded, but each of the operations is eternal. (*ST* I, 36, 3, ad 3)

But while Aquinas rightly holds that the Son is coeternal with the Father, he consistently argues, as noted on various occasions, that there is an order in that only what is first known can then be loved. This appears to undermine his statement that the Holy Spirit is coeternal with his principle, who is principally the Father, and in turn the Son, since the Father only loves the Son in the Holy Spirit only

therefore not be perichoretic-subsistent-relations-fully-in-act in a manner that properly constitutes the Trinity's eternity, for the Father only spirates the Spirit of Love as a sequential consequence of begetting his Son. The Father's eternity is the timeless act of begetting his Son and the distinct timeless act of loving his Son, that is, the timeless act that is the Holy Spirit. Likewise, the Son's eternity is the timeless act of loving his Father, that is, the timeless act that is the Holy Spirit. Thus, as stated previously, the Holy Spirit, as the Spirit of Love, timelessly brings to perfection, within their love for one another, the Father's fatherhood and the Son's sonship.

The conclusion to be drawn is that the term "eternity" demands that there is no "now," no "present" within the Trinity. Thus, as alluded to above, there is no "standing still now," wherein the persons of the Trinity know and love one another, for there is no eternal "moment" wherein they can do so. Because the Trinitarian act is one eternal, timeless perichoretic act wherein all of the persons of

---

"after" he knowns his Son. Thus this very sequential order, I believe, undermines Aquinas's affirmation that the Son does not exist prior to the Holy Spirit.

Now, while there is an order, that order must be properly understood. The Son does proceed from the Father, and the Holy Spirit does proceed from the Father and the Son, but that proceeding is not a sequential progression, as if only "after" the Father begets the Son does the Holy Spirit proceed from them as their mutual love. The order is that the Father is "first" named, for he, as the unoriginated plenitude of life and love, begets the Son, and the Son is "second" named because he is begotten of the Father in the Love that is the Holy Spirit, and the Holy Spirit is "third" named because he proceeds from the Father and the Son as their mutual inhering abiding Love. This numbering is not, then, by way of sequential progression, a succession from Father to Son to Holy Spirit, for the Father is defined by his begetting of his Son in the spirating of his paternal Love that is the Holy Spirit, and the Son is defined in his being begotten, a begetting wherein he, in union with the Father, co-spirates the Holy Spirit as his filial Love for his Father. The *order* must always be conceived within the *perichoresis* or *circumincessio*, the interrelationship between the three persons. Interestingly, Aquinas never employs the term *circumincession*, which may be the reason why he does not properly understand the *order* within the Trinity.

the Trinity are fully-in-act, within their perichoretic-relationships-fully-in-act, they are *fully present to one another* but not in a present. The very definition of who each is, in their singular identities, comprises their knowing and loving one another. Fatherhood-fully-in-act contains within itself the Father's timeless knowledge of and love for his begotten Son. Sonship-fully-in-act contains within itself the Son's timeless knowledge of and love for his Father. Love-fully-in-act contains within itself the Holy Spirit's timeless knowledge of and love for the Father and the Son, for he is the timeless perfect act of love that moves, and so brings to perfect form, the Father's paternal love for his begotten Son and the Son's filial love for his begetting Father. The persons of the Trinity "experience" no "now" within their relationships precisely because their relationships are singular in that they are fully in act and so timeless. That the persons of the Trinity are present to one another, but not in a "present," accentuates and heightens, and so properly defines, the eternality of their perfect fully enacted knowledge of and love for one another. Eternity unveils the metaphysical intimacy of the divine persons.

If there were a "now" within the Trinity, it would undercut the persons' fully-in-act-perichoretic-relationships whereby "eternity" defines their very essence. A "now" would insert an element of "time" into what, by definition, is timeless. Likewise, if there was a "present" within the Trinity, such a "standing still now" would also place the Trinity within a hierarchical order of being that would include "time-full" creation. The difference would be that while creation experiences the flow of time, the Trinity would not. Nonetheless, the Trinity would merely be at the apex of a hierarchical order of being and so would not exist in a manner that differs in kind, but only in degree, from that of creation. Instead of belonging to no genus, the Trinity would fall under the all-encompassing genus of "being," wherein it would simply be greatest within that order. The Trinity would then not exist in a manner that is ontologically singular, and so distinct from the order of time, that of creation. Because there is no "now" within the Trinity, however, timeless eternity defines the Trinity's essence.[14] The Trinity is its own eternity.[15]

14. Eleonore Stump and Norman Kretzmann are correct when they state that eternity "is misunderstood most often in either of two ways. Sometimes it is confused with limitless duration in time—sempiternality—and sometimes it is construed simply as atemporality, eternity being understood in that case as roughly analogous to an isolated, static instance." "Eternity," in *The Concept of God*, ed. Thomas V. Morris (Oxford: Oxford University Press, 1987), 219–20. Their essay was first published in the *Journal of Philosophy* 78, no. 8 (1981): 429–58.

They later argue, however, that "in some sense" there is a "present" in God, but "not a temporal present. And furthermore, the eternal, pastless and futureless present is not instantaneous but extended, because eternity entails duration" (225). Two comments are in order. First, while we conceive of eternity as duration—that is, everlasting existence—God does not experience his eternity as an everlasting duration, for, being eternal, his existence is timeless. Second, if God did experience eternity as an everlasting duration, then there would be an eternal present, and an ever-enduring eternal now, which I have argued is erroneous. I think Stump and Kretzmann want rightly to uphold that God is present to himself (or, in my thinking, that the persons of the Trinity are present to themselves) but in order for God to be present to himself, they believe he must possess a "present" wherein he experiences his presence (I wonder if here you could make a distinction between "existential presence" and "temporal presence." For the persons of the Trinity to be existentially present to one another, so to speak, there is no need for any kind of a "temporal presence." I think that's what you want to say.) What Stump and Kretzmann fail to grasp is that God, being eternally timeless, is present to himself but not in a "present." There is no eternal "now." I am confident that Stump and Kretzmann, in the light of this argument, would concede my point, for it upholds their primary concern. For a further critique of Stump and Kretzmann, see David Burrell, "God's Eternity," *Faith and Philosophy: Journal of the Society of Christian Philosophers* 1, no. 4 (1984): 389–406.

15. Again, Bonaventure addresses the issue of eternity within the context of the Trinity. For Bonaventure, God is eternal because he is simple and infinite. Being simple, God lacks a beginning and an end, and possesses total simultaneity. Because he is infinite, God is total interminability. "When both these attributes

I hope I have conceived correctly and articulated properly "eternity," as it defines the manner in which the Trinity exists.

---

are joined together, they constitute eternity. For eternity is nothing other than the 'simultaneous and total possession of interminable life'" (*Disputed Questions on the Mystery of the Trinity*, 5, 1, response). Bonaventure, like Aquinas, employs Boethius's definition of eternity. Because of the simultaneity of interminable life, Bonaventure, similar to Aquinas, speaks of an "eternal now" (5, 1, ad 13). But he also states that there is no "when-ness" in God, for he lacks a past and a future (see 5, 1, ad 5). Thus, while there is a "now" in God, for he is eternally present to himself, there is no "when-ness" in God, for he experiences no past and future. As I criticized Aquinas's use of Boethius's definition of eternity, so I would have the same concerns with regards to Bonaventure's.

Within these fundamental principles, Bonaventure concludes that the Trinity is eternal because, in its simplicity, it possesses infinite being. But eternity is more perfectly seen within the personal relations that constitute the Trinity. Although the relations within the Trinity distinguish the persons, these same relations constitute the Trinity's simplicity and simultaneity, for together they establish the oneness of the Trinity's eternal being. The Father's begetting of his Son and his breathing forth of the Holy Spirit does not, then, abolish simplicity within the Trinity. Rather, the Father's eternal begetting of his Son and his eternal breathing forth of his Spirit constitute the Trinity's simplicity, for the Father's "affections are turned to the good that is known and seen, so also the generation of the Word proceeding from the mind does not stand in the way of the breath of love which embraces both" (5, 2, ad 9). As we perceived previously, for Bonaventure, the ontological unifying principle that binds the Father and the Son together is the Love that is the Holy Spirit. Thus, for Bonaventure, the perichoretic interrelationship between the persons of the Trinity finds its terminus in the Love of the Holy Spirit. The Holy Spirit therefore completes or perfects, in their love for one another, the identities of the Father and the Son, and so completes or perfects their eternal perichoretic relations. The unity of love perfects eternity—the eternal ontological perichoretic embrace of the Father and the Son.

Only after he founds the Trinity's eternity on its simplicity and infinity does Bonaventure speak of the Trinity's highest immutability, an immutability that expresses the Trinity's full actuality (see *Disputed Questions on the Mystery of the Trinity*, 6, 1, response). "The supreme eternity is incompatible with any change; while supreme simplicity is incompatible with any possibility of change. Therefore, if the Trinity exists together with simplicity and eternity; and if there is no change where there is eternity and nothing capable of change where there is simplicity; and if every sort of mutuality is excluded where these are excluded, the Trinity and

Before proceeding to an examination of the notion of time as found within created reality, I want to make one important point— one that I made in the introduction to this book. In expounding various truths concerning the Trinity, it is readily apparent that we do not comprehend these very truths. We cannot intellectually grasp the manner in which the Trinity exists, even though we know that what is conceived and articulated must be the case. We do not comprehend what it means to be a subsistent-relation-fully-in-act, and so be the threefold act of pure being itself. Nor can we

---

supreme immutability necessarily exist together" (6, 1, response). "Furthermore, since actual immutability united with highest simplicity and eternity demands the highest actuality, and the actuality is realized in the full conversion of being itself upon itself in knowledge and love; and since understanding includes a word, and love includes union," it is proper that the Father, as the principle of knowing and loving, eternally "generates his Word and breathes forth Love. Both of these befit him immutably and actually at all times" (6, 1, response). Thus the Father, as the fully-in-act plentitude of life and love, speaks his living fully-in-act Word and breathes forth his fully-in-act Spirit of Love upon that Word. Again, for Bonaventure, it is the fully enacted, and so immutable, love of the Spirit that ontologically binds together the fully-in-act Father and the fully-in-act Word, thus completing and perfecting the eternal fully-in-act, and so immutable, Trinity.

Although I have been focusing exclusively on Aquinas's thought, Bonaventure, by placing the divine attributes—specifically simplicity, infinity, eternity, and immutability—within the context of the Trinity, has given these attributes a fuller and more proper meaning than does Aquinas, for the Trinity alone entails these attributes. Moreover, he has accentuated the essential role that the Holy Spirit, the Spirit of Love, plays within the Trinity, particularly in establishing the eternal perichoretic interrelationships wherein they constitute the one God. In both instances, what Bonaventure has done I have also attempted to do, though in a somewhat different manner, specifically in the Father begetting his Son in the Love of the Holy Spirit. I believe such an understanding would not only amend and so develop Aquinas's thought, but also enhance Bonaventure's.

Again, I want to thank Thomas Piolata for sending me his thesis. Some of what I have said above concerning Bonaventure I have garnered from his work, though in so doing I have attempted to fashion and enlarge it so as to develop my own thought. Piolata forced me to reread and rethink Bonaventure's *Disputed Questions on the Mystery of the Trinity*.

adequately imagine the perichoretic relationships between the Father, the Son, and the Holy Spirit wherein they are the one God. Nor can we conceive what it would be like to be an eternal being, though we must acknowledge that the persons of the Trinity exist in a timeless manner. Yet we know such to be true, for if such were not true, the Trinity, as revealed, would not be the Trinity. Thus we truly know what the mystery of the Trinity is, though we do not, and cannot, comprehend the mystery that we truly know. We know what is incomprehensible to us, and so we know what it is that we do not comprehend. This truthful knowing of the unfathomable will continue as we now examine the notion of time as found within creation and the manner in which time-full creation relates to the time-less Trinity.[16]

16. For further studies on eternity, particularly from within a Thomistic understanding and from the perspective of De Deo Uno, see R. Garrigou-Lagrange, *The One God* (St. Louis: Herder, 1943), 276–92; Paul Helm, *Eternal God: A Study of God without Time* (Oxford: Clarendon Press, 1988); M. J. Scheeben, *Handbook of Catholic Dogmatics, Book Two* (Steubenville, OH: Emmaus Academic, 2021), 133–45; E. Stump, *Aquinas* (New York: Routledge, 2003), 131–58; and E. Stump, *The God of the Bible and the God of the Philosophers* (Milwaukee: Marquette University Press, 2016), 56–75.

CHAPTER THREE

Time

Introduction

Now that we have examined the nature of God in his oneness
as pure act and that of the persons of the Trinity as subsistent-
relations-fully-in-act, and found that in both instances that the attribute of eternity pertains, by necessity, to their very manner of
existence, we need to determine the nature of time. In this short
but significant chapter, we see that "time" necessarily pertains to
the manner of creation's existence.

Time: The Enactment of the Future

When discerning, through the use of reason alone, whether God
existed and the manner in which he existed, we, in accordance with
Aquinas, first examined the nature of existing beings. We found
that while beings exist, nothing within their natures demanded
that they exist, nor are they capable of being the author of their
own existence. Such pertained not only to individual beings, but
also to the cosmos as a whole. Thus this contingent situation, where
beings exist whose natures do not demand that they exist and who

cannot account for their own existence, demands that there be a being who exists in and of himself—whose nature is being itself (*ipsum esse*), the pure act of being (*actus purus*). We also saw that the Father, the Son, and the Holy Spirit are perichoretic subsistent-relations-fully-in-act, whereby they exist as the one God. Thus the Trinity not only corresponds to what reason has concluded, that God is the pure act of being, but also it is the foundational reality that allows reason to make such a judgment. The nature of the Trinity's existence accounts for the necessity of its existence. Being subsistent-relations-fully-in-act, the persons of the Trinity are immutably perfect in their goodness, and as such they eternally exist in a timeless manner, for no further act could enhance the manner of their being. All of the above is in contrast to all else that exists. It is in contrasting the Trinity with all else that exists that we are able to establish the singularity of the Trinity's unique existence.

Although all finite beings exist in that they possess an act of existence, they, unlike the Trinity, are therefore not fully in act, for their natures inherently are in potency; that is, they are able to further enact their natures.[1] When addressing the difference between time and eternity, Aquinas states that while God is eternal in that

---

1. Within the created order, there is a hierarchy of being. Rocks, for example, exist, but because they are not living, they cannot further exact their existence. They may change because of the environment wherein they exist—wind and rain can change them, but they themselves are inert. Crystals are said to grow not because they are alive, but because they continuously add atoms, owing to the environment wherein they exist, such as mineral-rich water. While not living, stars, because of their gaseous makeup, continuously enact the star-ness. But living things change because they enact the potential contained within their respective natures. Trees continuously enact their tree-ness, and animals continue to exact their respective natures. Human beings consciously, knowingly, and freely enact their humanness, though at times in an evil manner. In enacting evil acts, they become less and not more human. Thus the whole of finite reality is in a constant state of change. In what follows, concerning the nature of time, I am primarily concerned with living beings.

he does not change, "time is the measure of movement," that is, the measure of the continuous progression of finite beings enacting the potential that resides within their natures. Other than the Trinity, all beings exist within an act and potency relationship. All beings progressively enact their potential and so continuously change.[2] Time marks the ever-progressive change that occurs within finite beings. Thus all finite beings, and the whole cosmos, are ever-progressing, in enacting their potential, from the past into the future. The important question is: What is the nature of the present, the "now," within this ever-progressing from the past to the future, the ever-occurring succession from one state of actuality to another state of actuality?

What is termed "the present" or "the now" is the act wherein a being enacts the future, and in so doing, the previous act of enacting the future becomes the past. Within finite reality, there is then no present as "present," nor is there a now as "now." What is perceived as the "present now" is always the enactment of the future. Time is always the progressive enactment of the future, wherein the former future becomes past and the "present-future" is enacted, only to become the past as the next future act is enacted. If there were a "present" as present and a "now" as now, it would mean that the being who enacted the "present" and so existed in a "now" had stopped enacting the future. This "stop-age," this "present-now,"

2. As is commonly acknowledged, changes within finite reality are either accidental or substantial. Accidental changes do not substantively alter the nature of the being, but rather change the nature such that it continues to be what it is. For example, a tree loses its leaves and grows new ones, while still remaining a tree. A crab sheds its shell and forms another, and continues to remain a crab. A person's hair can change from being black to gray, and they still remain who they are. A substantial change occurs when something ceases to be what it is and something of a different nature comes to be—stars burn themselves out; plants, animals, and human beings die. The remaining material is of a different nature, and so continues to change in accordance with what it now is.

would mean that the being is in a "standing-still-now" and so had fulfilled its potential. Having fulfilled its potential, it would finitely exist in a manner similar to how the Trinity exists in an eternal manner, in that both would be fully-in-act. But this "stop-age," this "present-standing-still-now," is impossible, at least in the cosmos as it now exists. Finite reality, by its very nature, is ever in a continuous enactment of the future, and every "now" is simply and only the progressive enactment of the future. Again, there is no now as a "now" within the finite order. For human beings, this absence of a "present" or a "now" has significant consequences.[3]

Now (pun intended—though note that "now" is alerting the reader to the next future word), neither the Trinity nor human beings experience a "present" or "now," though they experience this lack in a manner proper to who they are. Because the Trinity exists in a timeless manner, the divine persons do not experience a "present" or a "now." Human beings do not experience a "present" or a "now," for what they "now" experience is the continual enactment of the future. Such an experience of continuously enacting the future, of enacting what is potential, will only conclude upon their death.[4] Thus the duration of human life is a finite imitation, a

3. In his article "Temporal Integrity, Eternity and Implicate Order," Kenneth L. Schmitz provides a lengthy discussion of Edmund Husserl's phenomenological treatment of time. For Husserl, "the now is ... a sort of triad of duration; for it is that which is just-passing-away is still conjoined with the actual present, even while that which is not quite-yet is also conjoined with the same present." In *Beyond Mechanism: The Universe in Recent Physics and Catholic Thought*, ed. David L. Schindler (Lanham, MD: University Press of America, 1986), 106 (see also 105–10).

Although Husserl's phenomenological understanding of time may be similar to mine, he does not address the metaphysics behind such a phenomenological description. The reason that time is the ever-present enacting of the future, wherein the previously enacted future becomes the past, is that a living being is ever enacting its potential. In ever enacting its potential, a living being is ever entering into its future actualization.

4. I will elaborate on this point fully at the appropriate time.

finite replicating, of the Trinity. Although the persons of the Trinity are eternally fully in act, human persons, throughout the whole of their lives, are perfecting who they are as human beings. They are doing so by ever continuing to enact their human potential. Time, then, emulates or replicates eternity. Such an imitation should not be surprising, for it is from the timeless Trinity that human beings receive their time-filled existence. Thus, without eternity, there would be no time.[5] It is "existence" (*esse*) as "act" that constitutes this similitude between "eternity" and "time." The Trinity, being fully-in-act, is timeless. Human beings, being in act, are able, over the course of time, to enact their potential, ever becoming more perfectly who they are, and so imitate the perfect timeless Trinity from whom they received their existence.[6]

5. Once again, Thomas Piolata has pointed out that my understanding of time in relation to eternity is similar to Bonaventure's. In his introduction to Bonaventure's *Disputed Questions on the Mystery of the Trinity*, Zachary Hayes states, "Time itself [for Bonaventure] may be seen as a vestige of eternity; for present, past, future are so rooted in the fluid movement of time that what was future later becomes present and then past. If, on the other hand, the present were understood to be rooted in unchangeable and stable being, we would be approaching the meaning of eternity by negating the defects of the vestige." "Eternity is the mode of God's being as time is the creature's mode of being" (92). See Bonaventure's *Disputed Questions on the Mystery of the Trinity*, q. 5, a. 1, response.

6. Yet it is problematic to say, as I have just done, that human beings, in enacting their potential, are becoming ever more perfect. While such should be the case, it is not always the case, for, as already noted, they freely enact evil acts wherein they become less human. Also, they die not having completely perfected themselves. Therefore a few points need to be addressed not only concerning human beings, but also pertaining to the whole of finite reality. These comments are in anticipation of Part II of this study.

From within a Christian perspective, the good God created everything good, for he gave to everything the good gift of existence and a nature that, in itself, is a good thing to be. Because of sin, however, death entered the world. Thus God's good creation is now tainted and corrupted. Creatures, by nature, may have died prior to sin, but now death is perceived as an evil and, for human beings, a feared punishment. Although everything continues to possess the good of existence, the moral order, the order of right relationships, within creation is broken. Human beings no longer live in harmony with God nor with one another, nor with the rest of the created order. Human beings were made to live with the all-good and perfect God in an everlasting manner, but now their lack of goodness makes that humanly unattainable. The whole of God's revelatory saving acts, as found in the Old Testament, which find their fulfillment in the New Testament, establish a new salvific order wherein human beings, who abide within this salvific order, and the whole of creation can be made new, and so find their consummate perfection at the end of time. Literally, in the meantime, the whole of "creation waits with eager longing for the revealing of the sons of God," for then "creation itself will be set free from its bondage to decay and obtain the glorious liberty of the children of God." Until that time, the whole of creation is "groaning in travail," and not only creation, "but we ourselves who have the first fruits of the Spirit groan inwardly as we wait for adoption as sons, the redemption of our bodies" (Rom 8:19–23). For Christians, every successive present human enactment of the future is an act of groaning in the Spirit, an act that awaits the final act of their perfection. Moreover, although Christians continue to live in time, the time that they presently experience already contains within it an "eternal" quality, for they, in the eternal Spirit, already abide in the resurrected humanity Jesus, the eternal Son, and so abide with the eternal Father as his children. All of this will be developed further at the appropriate time.

CHAPTER FOUR

The Relationship between Eternity & Time

Introduction

Having examined the nature of time as the ever-progressing enactment of the future, the progression wherein potential is enacted, we must now examine the act of creation, for this act is the foundational act wherein the Trinity and the whole of creation are ontologically bonded together. Thus "eternity" and "time" are ontologically united. What is the nature of this union such that neither the manner of the Trinity's timelessness nor the manner of creation's time-fullness is jeopardized? Within the act of creation, the Trinity cannot become ensconced in time whereby it loses its timeless immutability, nor can creation become ensconced in eternity whereby its time-fullness becomes a chimera, an unreal illusion. Although the act of creation must ontologically unite the Trinity and creation, that very same act must maintain their distinct manners of existence—one as timeless and one as time-full.

The Act of Creation: A Mixed Relation

I believe, in considering the act of creation, sufficient attention has not been given to Aquinas's understanding of what is called a "mixed relation"—the kind of relationship that is established between God and creation within the creating act.[1] Understanding

1. In what follows, I summarize and develop within the context of the relationship between eternity and time what I have previously written in *Does God Change? The Word's Becoming in the Incarnation* (Still River, MA: St. Bede's, 1985), 88–96, and more fully in *Does God Suffer?* (Edinburgh: T&T Clark, 2000), 113–46. See also my "Aquinas: God *IS* Man—The Marvel of the Incarnation," in *Aquinas on Doctrine: A Critical Introduction*, ed. Thomas G. Weinandy, Daniel A. Keating, and John P. Yocum (London: T&T Clark, 2004), 67–89.

Since the above contains a rather extensive bibliography on the present subject, I will only note the more significant ones here, a few of which were published more recently. See D. Braine, *The Reality of Time and the Existence of God* (Oxford: Clarendon Press, 1988); D. Burrell, *Aquinas: God and Action* (London: Routledge & Kegan Paul, 1979); M. Dodds, *The Unchanging God of Love: Thomas Aquinas and Contemporary Theology on Divine Immutability* (Washington, DC: Catholic University of America Press, 2008); M. Dodds, *The One Creator God in Thomas Aquinas and Contemporary Theology* (Washington, DC: Catholic University of American Press, 2020); A. Krempel, *La Doctrine de la Relation chez Saint Thomas* (Paris: J. Vrin, 1952); M. Henninger, *Relations: Medieval Theories, 1250–1325* (Oxford: Clarendon Press, 1989); E. Muller, "Real Relations and the Divine: Issues in Thomas's Understanding of God's Relation to the Word," *Theological Studies* 56 (1995): 673–95; R. Neville, *God the Creator: On the Transcendence and Presence of God* (Chicago: University of Chicago Press, 1968).

Following Aristotle, Aquinas speaks of three kinds of relations (see *ST* I, 13, 7). First, there are "logical relations." These are made by and in the mind, such as relating Fido to the canine species. Because the relationship is mental and not within reality itself, they are often called "unreal relations." Moreover, within this mentally established relationship, neither term of the relationship is changed—Fido and the canine species are changed. Second, there are "real relations." These are established upon what is real within the two related terms, such as the parent/child relationship or husband/wife relationship. These relations are established by some mediating action that brings about a change within the terms related. For example, a man becomes a husband within the act of marriage, and similarly the woman becomes a wife. Likewise, these relations are expressed through mediating actions—hugs,

this relationship is essential for correctly perceiving the relationship between eternity and time. Aquinas most fully articulates this
Creator/creature relationship within the philosophical context of
the one God. I too will first address this relationship within that
context, but then I will place it within the fuller and more proper
context of the Trinity.

Because God is understood to be the pure act of existence,
ipsum esse, the act of creation is traditionally treated within this
setting, for what is to be given is being (*esse*) such that something
comes to be. The act of creation accentuates *that something is* rather than *what it is*.[2] Moreover, to bring something into existence
does not imply that "something" is changed, for "it" did not exist
prior to "its" creation.[3] Rather, the act of creation is an act that is
more dynamic than bringing about a change, for its effect is the
existence of the creature itself.

---

kisses, sexual acts. Of course, there can be real "hateful" relationships that express
themselves in angry words, punches in the nose, or slander. What needs to be noted is that "real relations" change the terms related. For Aquinas, the divine persons
possess real relationship with one another. They do so not in the sense that they
undergo change, but that they are truly constituted as who they are only in relation to one another (see *ST* 1, 28, 1). Third, there are relations wherein one term is
changed and the other term is not changed. Significantly, such relationships occur
when the terms do not exist in the same ontological order. For example, in coming
to know a tree, the person is changed from being "the non-knower" to becoming
"the knower," but the tree remains unchanged in being known. Thus the relation is
"mixed"—it is real in one term, for the knower is changed, but logical or unreal in
the other term, for the tree is unchanged. The act of creation establishes a "mixed
relation," for what is created comes to be by being "really" related to God, but God
is not changed in the act of creating and so is logically related to the creature—the
relationship is said to be "unreal" in God. We will now more fully discuss this
Creator/creature relationship, for it has frequently been misunderstood and misin-
terpreted. It should also be noted that the relationship between the divinity and humanity within the Incarnation is a "mixed relation." I will this treat more fully later.

2. See *ST* 1, 45, 4–6.
3. See *ST* I, 45, 1–3.

For Aquinas, the act of creation establishes a relationship between God the Creator and the creature, and this relationship is
signified differently, one that is proper to each of the two terms.
With regards to the creature, "Creation in the creature is nothing
but a certain relationship to the creator as to the principle of its
being."[4] Creatures are related to God as the source of the creature's
existence. Creatures are therefore related to God as God is as pure
being, for only in being related to God as God is do they exist.
With regards to God, "Creation signified actively means the divine
action, which is God's essence, with a relation to the creature."[5]
God acts by the pure act that he is, for no other act than pure act
could bring something into existence. Thus God is also related to
the creature, for through his creating act, he is the author of the
creature's existence, an existence that is founded upon the creature's
relation to him. God and creatures are, then, related *act to act*, that
is, the act of being by which a creature exists is related to the pure
act that God is, for in being related to the pure act that God does
the creature comes to be and continues to exist.

Nonetheless, the creature's relationship to God differs from
God's relation to the creature. "In God relation to the creature is
not a real relation, but only a relation of reason; whereas the relation of the creature to God is a real relation."[6] God's relation to the
creature is not real but is a relation of reason or a logical relation
since the act of creation does not change God, for he acts by his
essence, that is, by no other act than the pure act of being that he
is.[7] Thus the relation of the creature to God is termed "real," for

---

4. *ST* I, 45, 3.

5. *ST* I, 45, 3, ad 1.

6. *ST* I, 45, 3, ad 1.

7. Moreover, the act of creation itself demands such an act, for no other act
than the pure act of being is capable of such a singular act—*creatio ex nihilo*,
that of giving existence solely by the power of being pure being. While the act of

the relation constitutes the creature's being and continues to do so until it ceases to be.[8]

To designate God's relation to the creature as "unreal" or "logical" is not to attribute to God an absence, as if God were not closely related to the creature, or even that God is not *really* related to the creature in the sense of not being related at all.[9] Rather, for God to be the logical term of the Creator/creature relationship specifies the exact manner in which the creature is *really* related to him. The act of creation is that act whereby the creature is related to God not by some mediating act but by being related to God as God is in himself as pure being (*ipsum esse*). Therefore, for Aquinas, "as long as a thing has being, God must be most present to it; according to its mode of being. But being is innermost in each thing and most fundamentally inherent in all things since it is formal in respect of everything found in a thing. Hence it must be that God is in all things, and innermostly."[10] Unlike mutually "real" human relations, which are established by mediating acts, wherein human

---

creation demands that God act by no other act than pure act of being that he is, it is humanly impossible to conceive and comprehend how a pure act acts such that creatures come to be. The best that can be achieved is in knowing that in the act of creation, whereby God acts as the pure act that he is, creatures are related to God as he is as pure being (*ipsum esse*). Within that divinely enacted Creator/creature relationship, creatures come to be and continue to exist.

8. Creation and preservation are one and the same act. See *ST* I, 8, 1 and I, 9, 2.

9. Previously, I noted that the relationship between the knower and the known is a mixed relationship and gave as an example the knowing of a tree. Human beings are changed in knowing the tree, and so are really related to the tree. The tree, however, is not changed, and so the relationship is logical or unreal—a relation of reason. In this example, the tree does not "know" that the knower is related to it. In the Creator/creature relationship, however, while God is the logical term of the relationship, he is *actually* related to the creature, for the creature is *really* related to God. Moreover, God knows that he is *actually* related to the creature because the creature is *really* related to him.

10. *ST* 1, 8, 1. See also I, 8, 3, ad 1.

beings only partially give themselves to one another, such as in hugs and kisses, the Creator/creature relationship is founded, as stated above, upon an "act" to "act" relationship that is unmediated wherein the creature's act of being (*esse*) is immediately united to God as *ipsum esse*. Likewise, because the creature is related to God as God is, God himself is related to the creature as the creature truly is as a creature. Thus, because the creature is "really" related to God as God is, God, while being the logical term of the relation in that he does not change, is *actually* related to the creature in a manner that is absolutely immediate (no mediating act), supremely dynamic (pure act to created act), utterly intimate (a relation between God as he is in himself and the creature as it is in itself), and unbreakably enduring (it cannot be broken).[11]

To grasp the full significance of the act of creation as well as the relationship that is established between the Creator and cre-

11. Aquinas's critics consistently misunderstand his use of the term "unreal" or "by way of reason" when applied to God's relation to creatures. They interpret it as meaning nonexistent. Such an understanding is contrary to Aquinas's fundamental point. God is truly Creator because creatures are really related to him as he himself exists. When speaking of names for God, such as Creator, Savior, and Lord, Aquinas states that such titles "signify the action of God temporally" (*ST* I, 13, 7). Thus, "since God is related to the creature for the reason that the creature is related to him: and since the relation of subjection is real in the creature, it follows that God is Lord not in idea only, but in reality; for he is called Lord according to the manner in which the creature is subject to him" (*ST* I, 13, 7, ad 5). God in himself, from the very manner of his eternal being, is properly named Father, Son, and Holy Spirit, but he is named Creator, Savior, and Lord only in relation to what exists temporarily—only in the act of creation can God properly be called Creator, and only in saving humankind can he rightly be called Savior. Such names designate the manner in which temporal reality is related to God due to his divine action. For a more complete treatment of this issue and for a clarification of an ambiguity within Aquinas's thought, see my *Does God Change?*, 93–95, and *Does God Suffer?*, 136–37. To express the reality of God's relation to creation founded upon creation's "real relation" to God, I consistently employ the word "actual." God is *actually* related to creation because creation is *really* related to him.

ation within that act, we must now place our above understanding within the context of the Trinity. Only in so doing will we locate it within its proper setting, for it is the Trinity, and not simply the one God, who creates. Moreover, this Trinitarian context will bring to the fore a personalism that was previously lacking within the above philosophical treatment of God and the act of creation. We must remember that although the tradition rightly demands that all *ad extra* acts of the Trinity, those acts that result in effects outside itself, are done as one, the Trinity never generically acts simply as the one God. As stated previously, in the act of creation, God acts according to his essence, but to act according to "essence" is to act as a Trinity of persons, for the divine essence is the perichoretic interrelationship of the Father, the Son, and the Holy Spirit—the interrelatedness of the persons constitutes the divine essence or nature.[12] Thus to act as *ipsum esse* or as *actus purus* is for the persons of the Trinity perichoretically to act as subsistent-relations-fully-in-act, for these relationships constitute the pure act that each person distinctively is and are together.

In this light, Aquinas first argues that the act of creation is common to the whole Trinity.

Nevertheless, the divine persons, according to the nature of their procession, have a causality respecting the creation of things.... Hence also God the Father made the creature through his Word, which is his Son; and through his Love, which is the Holy Spirit. And so the processions of the persons are the type of the productions of creatures inasmuch as they include the essential attributes, knowledge and love.[13]

What Aquinas does not fully treat, probably because he felt he had adequately done so previously, is that the Trinity/creature rela-

12. See *ST* I, 39, 1 and I, 45, 3, ad 1.
13. *ST* I, 45, 6.

tion is a mixed relation. By not doing so, however, the Trinitarian personalism contained within the act of creation, that the Father creates through his Son in the Love of the Spirit, is not fully manifested.

Since the persons of the Trinity are subsistent-relations-fully-in-act, they possess no relational potential that requires further enactment in order for them to establish further relations. Thus the act of creation consists in relating the creature to themselves as they exist in themselves such that the creature comes to be. The creature is "really" related to the persons of the Trinity as they actually exist in themselves, and in so being related, the creature comes to be and continues to exist. For the persons of the Trinity to be the "logical" term of the creating act does not mean that they are not related to the creature. Rather, it specifies and accentuates that they, in not being changed in enacting the act of creation, are *actually* related to the creature, for the creature is *really* related to them as they exist in themselves, thus bringing the creature into existence. The act of creation therefore establishes an immediate, non-mediated, relationship between the persons of the Trinity and the creature. If the persons of the Trinity were not subsistent-relations-fully-in-act, creation could not be related to them as they exist in themselves. Moreover, the act of creation is, then, supremely dynamic, for the act by which the creature comes to be, its created *esse*, is the ontologically uniting of the creature to the fully-in-act persons of the Trinity. The act of creation establishes a singular "act" to "act" relationship—the act by which the creature exists and the perichoretic fully-in-act relations that constitute the persons of the Trinity. The act of creation is therefore also the most intimate, for the act of existence (*esse*) by which the creature comes to be is related to the persons of the Trinity as they exist in themselves as subsistent-relations-fully-in-act. Lastly, the act of creation establishes an enduring relation between the persons of the Trinity and the creature, for it lasts until the creature ceases to be, though human beings and angels never cease to be.

Now, specifically attending to each divine person, the Father, as the divine author of all that is, creates through his Word, for through his Word the Father not only knows himself, but he also knows the whole of creation.[14] For Aquinas, "Word implies relation to creatures. For God by knowing himself, knows every creature," thus "God by one act understands himself and all things, his one only Word is expressive not only of the Father, but of all creatures"[15]

Moreover, the Father enacts the act of creation through his Word, for in knowing the whole of creation in his Word, the Father creates all through his Word. Again, for Aquinas, the Father's Word is both "expressive" of what he knows and "operative" of what he creates.[16] Thus creatures, in being created by the Father through his Word, possess an unmediated relationship to the Word as the Word is, and so the creature is immediately related to the Father as the Father is, for the Word is the Father's knowledge of himself and all else that exists. The Father's act of creation through his Word establishes a relationship with creation that is, then, utterly dynamic and most intimate, for he knows creation in the very act of speaking his Word, and within that act of speaking his Word, he also freely creates all that exists. For human beings, this unmediated and intimate relationship that is established in the act of creation is inherently personal, for the human person is intimately related to the Word as the Word is and so is immediately related to the Father as the Father is. Human beings exist within a personal

14. The New Testament professes that God created all that is through his Word. See Jn 1:3, Col 1:16, 1 Cor 8:6, and Heb 1:2.

15. *ST* I, 45, 6.

16. *ST* I, 34, 3.

relationship with the persons of the Father and his Word as they perichoretically subsist in relation to one another.

Concerning the Holy Spirit, Aquinas states:

> The Father loves not only his Son, but also himself and us, by the Holy Spirit.... Hence, as the Father speaks himself and every creature by his begotten Word, inasmuch as the Word *begotten* adequately represents the Father and every creature; so he loves himself and every creature by the Holy Spirit, inasmuch as the Holy Spirit proceeds as the love of the primal goodness whereby the Father loves himself and every creature.[17]

As the Father knows the whole of creation within his spoken Word and so creates through his Word, so the Father loves, in the Spirit of Love, the whole of creation in loving his Son and so freely creates out of love for creation. Here, I want to accentuate, in accordance with my understanding of the processions within the Trinity, that as the Father begets his Son in the Love of the Spirit, so the Father, in the same Spirit in whom he begets his Son, lovingly creates through his Word. It is not that the Father first comes to know the whole of creation in his Word and in knowing creation loves it. Rather, as the Father begets his Word-known Son in the Love of the Spirit, so he creates his Word-known creation in the Love of the Spirit. As the Son proceeds from Father as begotten in the Spirit of Love, so in the act of creation, creatures come to be through the Father's Spirit imbued Word—the Spirit of Love in whom the Father, in his primal goodness, wills to create through his Word. Thus in the act of creation, creatures are immediately and intimately united to the Father's Spirit of Love as the Spirit of love is in himself, and as such, creatures are taken up into the very love that is shared between the Father and the Son. Creatures, in

17. *ST* I, 37, 2, ad 3.

coming to be and in continuing to exist, are related to the persons of the Trinity as they exist, whereupon the persons of the Trinity are actually related to the whole of creation. Such an understanding is accentuated when applied to human persons.

Because the persons of the Trinity are perichoretically subsistent-relations-fully-in-act, each possessing a distinct identity in relation to the other two, each human person, possessing a distinct identity, only exists in his or her distinctiveness by being related to each person of the Trinity in a manner that conforms to who the divine person distinctively is. The human person is personally related to the person of the Word/Son as the one through whom the Father creates the human person. Likewise, the human person is personally related to the person of the Holy Spirit as the one in whom the Father lovingly creates the human person through his Word. The human person is therefore personally related to the person of the Father as the author of the human person's existence, for the Father has created him or her through his Word/Son within his Spirit of Love. While remaining ontologically distinct, every human person is, in the Trinitarian act of creation, incorporated into the mystery of the Trinity itself—possessing a distinct relation with each divine person wherein the human person shares in their own perichoretic oneness. For Aquinas, then, the act of creation mirrors, though imperfectly, the processions within the Trinity.[18] "It is evident that relation to the creature is implied both in the Word and in the proceeding of Love, as it were in a secondary way, inasmuch as the divine truth and goodness are a principle of understanding and loving all creatures."[19]

18. See *ST* I, 45, 6, obj. 1 and ad 1.
19. *ST* I, 37, 2, ad 3.

The Trinitarian Act of Creation: Eternity and Time

Having examined the act of creation both as it pertains to the knowledge of God obtained by reason alone and as it pertains to the revealed Trinity, we can now place our understanding of the act of creation within the context of the relationship between eternity and time.[20] Now, the act of creation, as understood above, means that eternity as found timelessly within the Trinity of persons and time as found successively in creation are immediately, dynamically, intimately, and unbreakably related. Moreover, and of the utmost importance, the act of creation ensures that both eternity and time are not confused and not changed. The persons of the Trinity remain eternally who they are in themselves, and creation, within creation's real time, comes to be and exists. The full integrity of eternity and time are sustained, and for creation, time is properly constituted. Not only does the act of creation authenticate the unconfused and unchanged integrity of eternity and time, but it also, again significantly, ensures that eternity and time are not divided and not separated. The same act of creation that ensures the unchanged and unconfused integrity of eternity and time is the very same act whereby they are not divided or separated, for the act of creation not only constitutes creation's distinct reality from the Trinity, but it also constitutes its relationship to the persons of the Trinity. Thus creation's time and the Trinity's eternity are ontologically bound together in a manner that actuates the ontological distinctiveness of both while simultaneously authenticating their singular unity. Or, to put it differently, the very act of creation that

20. For the sake of unnecessary complexity, while what I will say pertains to what we know concerning God as found from reason alone, I focus exclusively on our understanding of the revealed Trinity.

ontologically distinguishes the Trinity's manner of existence from that of creation's manner of existence is the very same act that ontologically unites them. Creation ontologically distinguishes and ontologically unites eternity and time.[21]

The question that now arises is: How does creation's flow of time relate to the Trinity's timelessness, particularly concerning the Trinity's omniscience? As we saw, time is the measure of going from potency to act. The creature, in enacting its potential, undergoes change over the course of time. Since the Father, in an eternal timeless manner, knows every creature through his eternal and unchanging Word and loves every creature in his eternal and unchanging Spirit of Love, the changes that accrue to every creature over time do not effect a change within the Trinity itself. Nonetheless, over the course of time, the Trinity, within the Creator/creature relationship, is actually related to the creature because the creature is really related to the Trinity. Thus time-measured change remains within the created realm and is not assumed into the eternal realm of the Trinity, for if it did so, the Trinity would no longer exist in an eternal, fully actualized manner. Moreover, the eternal realm of the Trinity is not assumed into the realm of time, for if it did, the created realm of time would lose its created actuality. But how, then, can the Trinity be unchangeably omniscient, the eternal timeless knowing of all the changes that occur over the

21. In the above, I am obviously employing phrases taken from the Creed of the Council of Chalcedon (AD 451). The Council fathers were defining the relationship between the Son's two manners of existing—his two natures. In so doing, they recognized that the incarnational act, the "becoming," neither confuses nor changes the natures, for it is not a composition union of natures. Nor does the incarnational act separate or divide them, for it is the act whereby the human nature is united to the divine Son such that the Son comes to exist as man. As noted earlier, for Aquinas, the incarnational relationship, like the Creator/creature relationship, is a mixed relation. See my *Does God Change?*, 96–98, and *Does God Suffer?*, 206–8.

course of time? Would not the Trinity change in relationship to the changes that occur in time? In his *Summa Theologica*, Aquinas treats divine knowledge most extensively within the context of what reason alone discerns.[22] Taking into account his arguments and conclusions, I again place and develop them within the context of the Trinity.

As perichoretic subsistent-relations-fully-in-act, the Father perfectly knows himself and all else through Word—both of whom are constitutive of the unchanging divine essence.[23] Now, unlike human beings, who successively come to know objects outside themselves, the Father eternally knows himself and all else through his Word. Moreover, the Father, in knowing himself and all else through his Word, also knows the capacity to which his power extends, that is, all that he could do through his Word. The Father's power, as the fount of all existence, therefore extends to all that is created, for he, through his Word, is the efficient cause of all that exists.[24] Thus whatever effects preexist in the Father as the efficient cause must be eternally known by him in his Word.[25] The Father's knowledge through his Word therefore extends as far as his causality extends—that which could be, is, will be, or has been.[26] Thus what the Father knows through his Word he knows as the possible or actual cause of its existence. Nothing exceeds the Father's and Word's/Son's eternal omniscience, for all that the Father and Word/Son know, all that could possibly be known, is constitutive of their

22. See *ST* I, 14–16.
23. See *ST* I, 14, 2–4.
24. See *ST* I, 14, 7.
25. Although Aquinas speaks of God's knowledge as the efficient cause of creation, he also recognizes, as we have seen, that he does so by an act of the will (see *ST* I, 14, 8). Thus the Father creates through his Word, for he wills to do so in the Love of the Spirit.
26. See *ST* I, 14, 11.

very existence as Father and Son.[27] The manner of their existence and their manner of knowing are one and the same, for the Father and his Word/Son are perichoretically one as subsistent-relations-fully-in-act.[28]

Now, we cannot conceive the manner in which the Trinity is

27. For Aquinas, God's knowledge of all things is the cause of all things in a manner similar to that of an artist. The artist intellectually knows what he wishes to make, and so his knowledge is the cause of what he does make. God, in his omniscience, knows all that could possibly be, some of which he brings into existence (see *ST* I, 14, 8).

Brian Shanley provides a thorough presentation of Aquinas's understanding that God's efficient causality is the basis of his eternal knowledge of the temporal. See "Eternal Knowledge of the Temporal in Aquinas," *American Catholic Philosophical Quarterly* 71, no. 2 (1997): 197–224. Eleonore Stump and Norm Kretzmann take issue with Shanley's reading of Aquinas. They do not see God's causality as the basis of his eternal knowledge, for such would demand that God changes as creation progresses over time. Rather, God's omniscience is by way of eternal unchanging ideas. See "Eternity and God's Knowledge: A Reply to Shanley," *American Catholic Philosophical Quarterly* 72, no. 3 (1998): 439–45. As Shanley points out in his reply to Stump and Kretzmann, because these proposed eternal ideas are not founded upon God's efficient causality, there is no ontological basis upon which these eternal ideas are founded. There is an unbridgeable ontological chasm between God's purported omniscience and what actually temporally exists. See "Aquinas on God's Causal Knowledge: A Reply to Stump and Kretzmann," *American Catholic Philosophical Quarterly* 72, no. 3 (1998): 447–57. Moreover, as I have argued, the Creator/creature relationship as a mixed relation does not demand that God changes in relation to times progression, but rather that God's eternality is preserved as well as time's integrity.

From within the context of divine impassibility, for an excellent article on God's omniscience being founded upon his being the cause and sustainer of all that is, see James E. Dolezal, "Defending Divine Impassibility," in *Classical Theism: New Essays on the Metaphysics of God*, ed. Robert C. Koons and Jonathan Fuqua (London: Routledge, 2022).

28. See *ST* I, 14, 5. Aquinas argues that God knows all things in their particularity and not just in general, for not to know things in their particularity would be to possess a knowledge that is less than perfect (see *ST* I, 14, 6 and 11). Thus, for example, God knows each particular tree in its totality—whether it has existed, presently exists, or will exist in the future (see *ST* 1, 14, 9).

eternally omniscient. Aquinas speaks of God seeing all things together as one, which means that the Father, in knowing himself through his Word, knows all things in the one Word that Word is. Moreover, Aquinas speaks of God's "knowledge of vision." "Since God's act of understanding, which is his being, is measured by eternity; and since eternity is without succession, comprehending all time, the present glance of God extends over all time and to all things which exist in time, as to objects present to him."[29] Because the persons of the Trinity exist in a timeless manner, they experience no sequential movement. Rather, their knowing vision encompasses all time and so all that exists in time. The reason is that all that exists, will exist, or has existed is present to the persons of the Trinity, and so the divine persons are present to them in accordance with their present existence, future existence, or past existence. Such an understanding, ironically, may be more clearly seen within the context of the Trinity knowing future contingencies, a conundrum that philosophers and theologians have continually attempted to fathom.

Because the persons of the Trinity are omniscient, they know all that is possible, including future contingents, that is, a state of affairs that need not exist but will actually come to be.[30] Human beings have no certain knowledge of what could be—the future. But Aquinas argues that God knows contingencies, for he knows the causes by which they will become actual. For example, the divine

29. *ST* I, 14, 9.
30. For an excellent study on God's omniscience and future contingents, see Harm J. M. J. Goris, *Free Creatures of an Eternal God: Thomas Aquinas on God's Infallible Foreknowledge and Irresistible Will* (Nijmegen: Thomistic Institute of Utrecht, 1996). See also James K. Beilby, K. James, and Paul R. Eddy, *Divine Foreknowledge: Four Views* (Downers Grove, IL: InterVarsity, 2001); William Hill, "Does God Know the Future? Aquinas and Some Moderns," *Theological Studies* 36 (1975): 3–18; Shanley, "Eternal Knowledge."

persons, unlike the weatherman, eternally know for certain that it will rain at a particular time because they know the atmospheric conditions that will cause it to rain. Similarly, the divine persons eternally know what free choices a human person will make, for they eternally know that particular human person who will make those free choices.[31] Thus, while contingences successively come to actuality, the persons of the Trinity, because they are subsistent-relations-fully-in-act, know such actualized contingencies in a timeless manner, for all that takes place in time is present to the divine persons in an eternal timeless manner, within their eternal omniscient vision that encompasses the whole of time. Significantly, if God had "a present," our past, present, and future would be his past, present, and future. But since God is timeless and so possesses no present, he knows our past, present, and future as ours and not his. While we speak of God's foreknowledge, as if he knew "the future" as future, he does not know "the future" as future, for there is no "future" in God. Rather, in a timeless manner, he knows "the future as creation's future" and not his own. Thus he knows future contingencies as creation's future contingencies, an unknown future that pertains to creation and not to himself.[32] In this context,

31. See Psalm 139, where the Psalmist expresses God's omniscient knowledge of the human person's actions.

32. Many authors have judged that there is a "present" in God, an eternal "now." Because of this conviction, the issue concerning God's eternity in relation to time, particularly his knowledge of contingent future events, remains an unfathomable riddle. As stated above, if God is present to himself in a "present," then the flow of time necessitates that there resides a past, present, and future within that divine "present." If there is a "future" residing within the divine "present," then the issue of God knowing contingent future events not only becomes an insoluble problem but also becomes, as many scholars have argued, contradictory. God cannot be both eternally and immutably omniscient and equally know what is contingently yet to be enacted. I think this is evident, for example, within the many influential writings of Eleonore Stump and Norman Kretzmann. They wish to maintain that God knows future contingents in an omniscient and immutable manner, yet because

Aquinas importantly states that God eternally knows all things as they are "in their presentiality (*praesentialitate*)."[33] This concept of "presentiality" is significant—at least I believe my interpretation of it is significant.

"Presentiality" must be understood within the context of the relationship that is established between God and the creature in the act of creation—that is, a mixed relation. As we saw, within this relationship the Trinity is *actually* related to the creature, for the creature is *really* related to it. Now, the Father eternally knows all in knowing himself in his Word, and all is therefore eternally present to the Father in his Word. Moreover, the Father, through the Holy Spirit, eternally loves all that he knows. There is an eternal "presentiality" of knowledge and love. When a creature comes to be and so is related to the Trinity as the Trinity is, that creature is present to the Trinity in a new manner—as existing. While there is no change in the Trinity through this new present relationship, because the creature is newly related to the Trinity, the Trinity is *actually* related to it in a new manner. Thus the Trinity knows and loves the creature in its new "presentiality"—as an existing creature, and it does so not because there is a change in manner in which the Trin-

they hold that there is, in some sense, a "present" in God, they struggle mightily to provide a convincing argument. As I maintain, however, there is no "present" in God. Because God is present to himself but not in a "present," his omniscience does not contain an "experience" of a past, present, or future. He knows all in knowing his immutable, eternally timeless self. See Norman Kretzmann, "Omniscience and Immutability," *Journal of Philosophy* 63 (1966): 408–21; Eleonore Stump and Norman Kretzmann, "Eternity," in *The Concept of God*, ed. Thomas V. Morris (Oxford: Oxford University Press, 1987), 219–52, and Eleonore Stump and Norman Kretzmann, "Eternity, Awareness, and Action," *Faith and Philosophy: Journal of the Society of Christian Philosophers* 9, no. 4 (1992): 463–82. Paul Helm appears to hold a view similar to my own. See his *Eternal God: A Study of God without Time* (Oxford: Clarendon Press, 1988), 36–37, 98–101.

33. *ST* I, 14, 13.

ity eternally knows and loves, but because there is a newness in the manner in which the existing creature is now present to the Trinity. Moreover, then, as the creature continuously enacts the future, and so its potentiality, it is ever, within the flow of time, newly related to the Trinity as the Trinity is, and so the Trinity is ever present to the creature's ever-changing presentiality. The persons of the Trinity are ever present to the creature in the manner in which the creature presently exists. In being present to the creature in the manner in which the creature presently exists, the persons of the Trinity continuously know and love the creature as the creature is, not because their knowledge and love of the creature has changed, but because the creature has changed in relation to them. Thus the persons of the Trinity are most presently present to the creature throughout the course of the creature's ever-changing present—its continuous enactment of the future. The persons of the Trinity possess an immediate, intimate, and dynamic knowledge and love of the creature, and thus of the whole of the created order as well. Such divine knowledge and love are especially relevant to human beings. The person of the Father immediately and intimately knows, in his personal love that is the Holy Spirit, each human person in the person of his Word/Son. Throughout the course of time and beyond death, there is a personal relation, founded upon the act of creation, between the Trinity and the human person, one in which the Father, in a timeless manner, knows in his Word and loves in his Spirit the human person. The Father eternally knows in his Word and loves in his Spirit the human person as the person "is" within the flow of time, for the human person is, in his or her presentiality, always related to the Trinity as the Trinity eternally and unchangeably is. Such a personal relationship is, again, founded upon the act of creation. It is a metaphysical reality.

At this juncture, we must acknowledge the fact that the relationship between God and creation, between eternity and time, was disrupted by sin. Although the Trinity created everything good, human beings, in their freedom, rebelled against God by disobeying his command in their arrogant desire to be divine-like themselves. In his mercy, God set out to re-create humankind. In so doing, he established a new salvific relationship between himself and those who enter into his saving work through faith. This new relationship, by its very nature, reordered the relationship between eternity and time, for those who abide in this new relationship with God enter into the very life of the Trinity itself and share in their eternal nature. Time, then, becomes divinized. To this salvific relationship and its implications for eternity and time we now turn in Part II of our study.

Part II

———

Besides the metaphysical reality founded upon the act of creation, there also ensues, within the relationship between the Trinity and humankind, a moral component. This personal relationship of knowing and loving may not be reciprocal on the part of the human person. By way of divine revelation, we know that the primordial human couple (biblically named Adam and Eve) freely sinned against their good and loving Creator, and in so doing became, because of their sin, morally estranged from the Trinity. Although the Trinity, as the Creator, continued to know and love humankind, humankind no longer knew and loved the Trinity as originally intended. Ontologically, human beings and all of creation continue to possess the good of existence, yet human beings and the whole of creation were now marred by sin with its curse of death. Time, then, marks not only the enactment of good deeds, but also the enactment of evil deeds. What is then needed is for the Trinity to make new, morally re-create, the sin-fallen creation, and so redeem time.

CHAPTER FIVE

The Salvific
Relationship between
Eternity & Time

Introduction

History, from within a Jewish/Christian perspective, is not simply the recording of the relationship between the Trinity as Creator and the created realm, particularly with human beings, and thus the relationship between the Trinity's eternity and creation's time. It is also the history of sin and redemption. It is the history of the Trinity's saving actions within time whereby human persons, and the whole of creation, are freed from the moral decrepitude of sin with its curse of death. Moreover, these Trinitarian actions establish a new relationship with human beings wherein they are made holy and so are taken up into the very life of the Trinity. Thus the relationship between eternity and time, the relationship between the Trinity and human beings, is enhanced—time is redeemed by assuming characteristics of eternity's divine disposition. Although the metaphysical relationship between eternity and time, as founded upon the act of creation, has been extensively treated, to my knowledge the salvific relationship between eternity and time has not been treated. Thus I hope that the following will contribute to a fuller understanding of the relationship between eternity and time and so address, at least partially, this lacuna.[1]

One further introductory point, which is of the utmost importance, must also be made. In his immanent revealing salvific acts within time and history, God manifests that he exists in a manner that transcends the created order of time and history. Only if God exists outside the created order of time and history could he perform the saving revelational acts that he does perform. Moreover, his salvific acts in time and history do not jeopardize God's transcendent eternal manner of existing. This is the primary, central, and pivotal mystery of biblical revelation and of the Jewish/Christian faith. Although this mystery is first evident within God's saving and covenantal acts as found in the Old Testament, it is supremely manifested in the Incarnation. The Son of God, who exists in an eternal manner, truly comes to exist as man in a timely manner, and he does so without jeopardizing his eternal divine manner of existence. He who is consubstantial (*homoousion*) with the Father as the Father's Son is the same Son who is consubstantial (*homoousion*) with human beings as they are human. Jesus is truly the Son of God truly existing as truly man. Thus, within the incarnational reality, the eternal Son of God never acts in time in a divine manner, but he always lives and acts in a time-full human manner. Such is the case both in performing miracles or in eating a piece of bread.[2]

---

1. I will not attempt to provide a theological account of the Trinity's saving acts but rather a summary overview, in broad strokes, of what is often referred to as the history of salvation. For a more detailed account, see my *Does God Suffer?*, 214–42.

2. For a fuller theological and philosophical development of this understanding of God's immanent saving acts within time and history by which he manifests his wholly transcendent eternal otherness, see my *Does God Suffer?*, 40–63.

The Old Testament: The Anticipatory Acts of Time's Redemption

The Book of Genesis declares the goodness of God's creation, and so the evil that is now found within it is not due to some malevolent creator deity or from matter as found within other ancient mythical creation stories.[3] The created realm is ontologically good and not evil in itself. Rather, evil entered the world through the misuse of human freedom—Adam and Eve, in their desire to be like God, disobeyed his commandment. They ate of the tree of knowledge of good and evil.[4] The effect of this primordial sin had a fourfold effect. First, sinful humanity was alienated from the all-holy God, as found in Adam's hiding from God. Second, human relationships were also impaired, as witnessed in Adam and Eve realizing they were naked, and in the woman's desire for man, and yet his rule over her. Third, the primordial sin put in motion the proliferation of sin within history, and human beings were now prone to sin, as first found in Cain killing Abel.[5] Their morally compromised hearts and minds were no longer focused on doing what is good. Lastly, creation itself was marred. Women would now bear children in pain. Moreover, unlike in Eden, the garden of Paradise, wherein there was an abundance of food, man would now till the cursed ground amid thorns and thistles and eat bread by the sweat of his brow. Humankind will experience or do all of this until it returns to dust, the dust from which it came.[6]

Now, humankind is incapable of rectifying the sinful situation in which it now finds itself. Only God can restore it to its divine

3. See Gn 1:1–31.
4. See Gn 3:7.
5. See Gn 4:8–16.
6. See Gn 3:1–19.

likeness and so reestablish a holy relationship with him by making
human beings once more holy. The whole of the Old Testament is
the history of God's initial redemptive acts, anticipatory acts that
prophetically prefigure his ultimate saving acts. Such acts begin
with the historical calling of Abraham. Abraham will be the father
of a great nation, and in him all nations will be blessed.[7] As God's
chosen people, the Israelites have a relationship with God that differs in kind from his relationship with all of the other nations, a
relationship that exceeds that of the Creator/creature relationship.
This covenantal relationship was enhanced when, having freed the
Israelites from Egypt, God (YHWH) made a covenant with Moses and the people at Mt. Sinai. Taking the blood of an ox, Moses
sprinkled the blood on the altar and upon the people, the blood
that signified that the Israelites and God, by means of the covenant,
shared the same common life together. To be faithful to the covenant, the people were to keep the Ten Commandments and other
divine ordinances, for in doing so they would be God's holy people,
and he would be their all-holy God.[8] Thus, because of their covenantal relationship with the all-holy God, Israel would be a holy
nation, a nation separated from the other profane and irreligious
nations. They were to be holy as the Lord their God is holy.[9] What
we perceive in the above summary account is God acting in such
a manner that Israel, becoming his chosen covenantal people, possesses a relationship with God wherein their ensuing history, their
time, is sanctified, for they are conjoined to the eternal manner in
which God exists as all-holy. Such sanctified time is evident not
only in that God dwells in their midst and resides in their Jerusa-
lem temple, but more specifically in the yearly round of holy days

7. See Gn 12:1–3.
8. See Ex 6:7 and 24:3–8.
9. See Ex 19:5–6 and Lv 21:8.

and liturgical feasts they observe—the holiest being Passover, the remembrance, the making present, of God freeing them from the slavery of Egypt and his making of the covenant with them. In that Passover Covenant, God sanctified Israel's history, a history that is annually renewed every *time* it is celebrated.

Now, in returning to what was discerned in our discussion of the Creator/creature relationship, the covenantal relationship that God established with his chosen people, and in their faithfulness to his commands with their annual ensuing liturgical feasts, God does not change. His timeless manner of being remains immutable. Because of the covenant, however, the Israelite's relationship to God has changed. Because they are *really* related to God in a covenantal manner, God is *actually* related to them in a covenantal manner. Thus, over the historical flow of time, the Israelites, in their presentiality, are ever newly present to God, and so God, in his omniscience, is ever newly present to them and so knows them ever newly through the course of time. This "newness" is due not by way of a change in God, but in the ever-new timely manner in which the Israelites are present to him.[10]

The issue that obviously arises is that Israel is not faithful to God's covenant. The Old Testament is not only the history of God acting on behalf of and in the midst of his people; it is equally a history of Israel's infidelity—a history of not keeping God's commandments and ordinances, a history of worshiping false gods. This infidelity brings to light a deeper issue. Although the covenant did establish a unique relationship between God and his people, with the intention of sanctifying their time-bound relationship with him, it did not adequately interiorly transform them. Their

10. While I am speaking of the Israelites as a whole, as a covenanted people, individual Israelites will be related to God in accordance to their faithfulness or unfaithfulness to the covenant. The sinfulness of Israel will be discussed immediately.

interior transformation, their being re-created and made new, was not effectively achieved. God himself addresses this inadequacy as found in the prophetic books.

For example, speaking on God's behalf, Jeremiah declares:

> Behold, the days are coming says the Lord, when I will make a new covenant with the house of Israel and the house of Judah, not like the covenant which I made with their fathers when I took them by the hand to bring them out of land of Egypt, my covenant which they broke, though I was their husband says the Lord. But this is the covenant which I will make with the house of Israel after those days, says the Lord: I will write it upon their hearts; and I will be their God, and they shall be my people.[11]

God will not write this promised new covenant on tablets of stone, as he did in the past, but within the very hearts of his people. This interior inscription implies a recreation. Because of this interior transformation by which his people will be empowered to live faithful holy lives in communion with their all-holy God, God will truly be their God, and they will truly be his people. God articulates more fully the particulars of this new covenant through the prophet Ezekiel.

The exiling of God's people to Babylonia manifested their sinful unholiness. This manifestation negatively redounded back to God, giving the impression that he was not holy enough to make his people holy. Thus, for his sake, and not for the sake of his people, God will make them holy so as to vindicate his holy name before the very eyes of all the nations.

> I will sprinkle clean water upon you, and you shall be clean from all your uncleannesses, and from all your idols I will

11. Jer 31:31–33.

cleanse you. A new heart I will give you, and a new spirit I will put in you; and I will take out of your flesh the heart of stone and give you a heart of flesh. And I will put my spirit within you, and cause you to walk in my statues and be careful to observe my ordinances. You shall dwell in the land which I gave to your fathers; and you shall be my people, and I will be your God.[12]

In order to vindicate his holy name, God will do three things. First, in sprinkling his people with clean water, he will purify them of their sin and cleanse them of the idols. Second, he will remove their heart of stone and give them a new heart of flesh, and in so doing, he will place his very own divine spirit within them in order to empower them to keep his commandments; thus God will interiorly re-create them and make them new. Last, in returning to the land that God gave to their fathers, they will once more truly become God's people, and God will manifest that he is truly their God.

What is evident from what God speaks through the prophets Jeremiah and Ezekiel (and other prophets as well) is that he recognizes the inadequacy of solely providing covenantal commandments and precepts. There also needs to be a corresponding act of re-creation, for without this re-creating act, his people were incapable of keeping the covenant. God obviously knew from eternity that his people would not and could not keep the covenant he made with them. In the peoples' failure to keep the covenant, God was teaching them the depth of their fallenness and the dire need for them to be re-created. Thus, when God prophesies the coming of his new covenant, one in which his people would be interiorly renewed by his abiding spirit, they themselves would clearly recognize their urgent need for salvation. This salvific need gives rise to

12. Ezek 36:22–28.

God's promise to send, and the peoples' expectation to receive, the long-awaited Messiah, a Spirit-filled savior.

In this light, we perceive, as did the Israelites themselves, that the initial covenant was a prophetic anticipation of what would be fulfilled in the new covenant that was to come. Although God's initial covenant did effect a new relationship between God and his people, one in which their history became a sacred history, a history that was celebrated in an annual timely manner within their liturgical feasts, particularly the Passover, it did not effect a re-creation of God's people, and so they were incapable of being holy as the Lord their God is holy. Therefore their lives, and so their history, were not fully sanctified. Their liturgical temple sacrifices were temporal prophetic harbingers of what was to come. Time is yet to be redeemed and so deified.

Now, with the coming of the Messiah and the re-creation he will achieve, he will make possible a new relationship, a new covenant, between God and his people. If the former covenant sanctified, and continues to sanctify, Israel's history, the new covenant will do so in a new manner, for the people will themselves, in being re-created, be untied to God in a new manner—one in which they, and all nations, will be able to be deified and so abide within the Trinity itself.

The Incarnation: The Binding Together of Eternity and Time

It was noted at the onset of this section that in the incarnating act, in the incarnational "becoming," it is truly the Son of God who truly comes to exist as a true man. Although incomprehensible, this incarnating act finds clarity when placed within the context of a mixed relation. As was already argued with regard to the act of creation, the persons of the Trinity are subsistent relations fully in act. As such, they possess the singular ability to unite, as in the act of creation, "something" to themselves as they exist in themselves. Similarly, in the incarnating act, what is enacted by the Holy Spirit in the womb of Mary is the bringing into existence the humanity along with the simultaneous uniting of that humanity to the person of the Son such that the Son comes to exist as man.

Now, the humanity is *really* related to the person of the Son, for it comes to be and is united to the person of the Son as the Son actually exists as God. Because the humanity is united to the Son as he eternally exists as God, the Son is *actua*lly united to his humanity. Given that the humanity is united to him as he eternally exists in his immutable divine nature, the Son does not change. If he did change in being so united, he would no longer be the eternal Son of God, but some lesser divine expression of himself. Likewise, in being united to the person of the Son, the humanity is not changed, since it comes to be and remains what it is within the incarnational union. In this incarnating act, there is, then, the ultimate binding together of eternity and time. This incarnational union of eternity and time undermines neither the Son's eternal timeless existence nor his earthly human time-full existence. In accordance with the Council of Chalcedon, neither eternity nor time is jeopardized, for the incarnational union is not the compositional union of natures, wherein they would be confused or changed, thus amalgamating eternity and time, where both would lose their integrity. Moreover, eternity and time are neither divided nor separated, for the two manners of the Son's existence, that of being God and man, are united to the one person of the Son such that the eternal Son actually exists timely as man.[13]

13. For a more extensive treatment of the Incarnation as a mixed relation, see my *Does God Change?*, 96–100; *Does God Suffer?*, 206–8, and "Aquinas: God *IS*

Such a Chalcedonian understanding, while expressing the supreme mystery, preserves the truth that Jesus is truly the eternal
Son of God truly existing as truly man and so within the confines
of time. The Incarnation is, then, the foundational mystery wherein
history can be sanctified, and time can be deified in that human
beings can be subsumed into this incarnational mystery. Moreover,
this subsuming of human beings into eternity can only be achieved
through the human, timely saving actions that Jesus performs
as the Father's incarnate Spirit-filled Messianic Son. Here, a full
theological exposition of Jesus' salvific acts cannot be expounded.
Nonetheless, a summary overview is essential.

The New Passover Covenant:
The Deification of Time

As prophetically anticipated in the Passover covenantal act as nar-
rated in the Old Testament, Jesus' sacrificial death on the cross
is the supreme efficacious act wherein the new and everlasting
Passover covenant is established. Jesus, as the perfect Spirit-filled,
all-holy high priest, offers himself as the perfect Spirit-filled,
all-holy sacrifice. Jesus does so in perfect love for his Father and
in his perfect love for sinful humankind. Jesus, then, is the true
Lamb of God who takes away the sin of the world.[14] This sacrifice
redeems, sets free, humankind from sin, and so reconciles humankind to the Father. Moreover, in this new and everlasting covenantal Passover sacrifice, Jesus merits his resurrection—his passing
over from death to everlasting life. His Father confirms the salvific

Man—The Marvel of the Incarnation," in *Aquinas on Doctrine: A Critical Introduction*, ed. Thomas G. Weinandy, Daniel A. Keating, and John P. Yocum (London:
T&T Clark, 2004), 67–89.

14. See Jn 1:29.

efficaciousness of Jesus' sacrifice by gloriously raising him from the dead. Thus the resurrected Jesus himself embodies the fruit of his own saving work—"he is the first born from the dead."[15]

Now, although Jesus' sacrificial death on the cross was humanly enacted in time, the Father's reciprocal act of raising Jesus gloriously from the dead actualized an effect wherein the human resurrected Jesus is now related to his Father in a manner that differs from his previous pre-resurrected incarnate state. The bodily risen Jesus presently exists within the eternal, and so timeless, realm of his heavenly Father. Although he no longer lives within earthly time, Jesus, as a risen man, obviously does not acquire the Father's timelessness in a divine manner. He lives in a manner wherein he has assumed attributes, as analogously appropriate and conformable to human beings, that apply to the Trinity's eternal manner of existence.

The term "gloriously," as employed in the preceding paragraph, is an attempt to express this changed mode of existence. When the risen Jesus appeared to Mary Magdalene and to his disciples, he did so as a physical human being, such that he could be touched and in a manner wherein he could eat a piece of fish. His physical body also bore the recognizable marks of his crucifixion. Yet he could physically appear and disappear at will, and he could enter rooms whose doors were bolted. Thus, although Jesus manifested an authentic physicality, his physical humanity was radically different from other earth-bound human beings. By ascending into heaven, the risen Jesus revealed that he presently lives in a heavenly manner, that is, his being humanly assumed into communion with his heavenly Father. He no longer resides in the earthly realm of time but in the heavenly realm of eternity, and so in a manner that remains inexplicable.

15. Col 1:17.

CHAPTER SIX

The Glorification of Jesus & His Disciples

Introduction

To appreciate fully what it means for Jesus, through his salvific work, to be glorified, we need to examine John's Gospel and Paul's teaching. Only by grasping the manner in which Jesus is glorified through his death and resurrection are we able to perceive the manner in which Christians are gloried in Christ, both in this *time-bound* life and at the end of *time* when they assume the fullness of Jesus' *eternal* risen glory.

John's Gospel

Interestingly, John's Gospel does not narrate Jesus' Transfiguration. The reason for this absence is that his entire Gospel is the narrative of Jesus manifesting his ever-progressing glorification. "And the Word became flesh and dwelt among us, full of grace and truth;

we have beheld his glory, glory as the only begotten Son from the Father."[1] From all eternity, the only begotten Son possessed the totality of his Father's divine glory, for he is God as the Father is God.[2] This eternal divine glory is now manifested through the Son's humanity—his human existence. Initially, this glory was seen in Jesus' miracles, signs of his glorious divinity.[3] Jesus' glory comes to its completion within his death and resurrection—the twofold hour of his glory. In his high priestly prayer, Jesus prays:

> Father, the hour has come; glorify your Son that the Son may glorify you, since you have given him power over all flesh, to give eternal life to all whom you have given him. And this is eternal life, that they know you the only true God, and Jesus Christ whom you have sent. I glorified you on earth, having accomplished the work which you gave me to do; and now Father, glorify you me in your own presence with the glory which I had with you before the world was made.[4]

Jesus, the incarnate Son, prays that the Father would glorify him so that he would be able to glorify his Father, that is, that the Father would glorify him in his crucifixion and death, so that in his crucifixion and death he would glorify his Father. The goal of Jesus' crucifixion and death, the mutual glorification of the Father of his Son and of the Son of his Father, is that of bestowing eternal life upon all whom the Father has given to him. Eternal life consists in knowing the Father as the one true God and his Son, Jesus Christ, the one whom the Father sent to accomplish his saving work, a work that he is now about to complete.

1. Jn 1:14.
2. See Jn 1:1–5.
3. See Jn 2:11.
4. Jn 17:1–5.

Moreover, if the Father glorifies Jesus in his crucifixion and death, then the Father will also glorify him in his presence through the Father raising him gloriously from death. In doing so, Jesus, the risen incarnate Son, will enjoy the same glory that he eternally possessed before the foundation of the world. Thus the fruit of Jesus' saving death and resurrection, the consequence of the mutual glorification of the Father and the Son, is that those who come to know, in faith, the Father and his incarnate Son will share in their eternal glory. They too will participate in the divine life that singularly bears the attribute "eternal," for they will abide with the eternal Father as his Spirit-filled children. They will do so because they are in communion with his risen and glorious incarnate eternal Son, Jesus Christ. Thus Jesus prays on behalf of his disciples: "The glory which you have given to me I have given to them, that they may be one even as we are one, I in them and you in me, that they may become perfectly one."[5] By sharing in Jesus' risen glory, his disciples become one as he and his Father are one, for Jesus, the risen incarnate Son, abides in them and the Father abides in him. This mutual divine abiding is what makes Jesus, his Father, and Christians perfectly one.

Furthermore, this perfect divine oneness manifests that the Father loves Jesus' disciples "even as you have loved me."[6] Jesus therefore desires that his disciples be with him where he is so that they may see his divine glory and so come to share in his glory. Jesus has revealed to his disciples his Father, and he assures his Father that he will continue to do so "that the love with which you have loved me may be in them and I in them."[7] As Jesus, the Father's Son, shares in his Father's eternal divine glory, so he equal-

5. Jn 17:22–23.
6. Jn 17:23.
7. Jn 12:25–26.

ly shares in his Father's divine love. By making his Father known to his disciples, they too come to share in the same eternal love that the Father has for him. In this mutual sharing of the Father's eternal love, Jesus abides in them, and in him they abide with his Father. To be taken up into the very life of the Trinity, to partake in their divine attribute of "eternity" in a manner that is appropriate to being human, is the goal of the Father's salvific work, a work that Jesus achieved through his death and resurrection. Thus the relationship between the Trinity and Christians differs in kind, and not simply in degree, from that of the primordial Creator/creature relationship, for Christians actually come to abide within the Trinity itself.

Paul's Teaching:
Becoming Imperishable and Immortal

Paul, in his First Letter to the Corinthians, provides the fullest attempt at explaining what it means to be gloriously risen, but one senses that he is rather agitated in his endeavor to do so. He recognizes that what he says cannot adequately address the topic. Importantly, his explanation takes into account both Jesus' resurrection and the resurrection of those who believe in him. Having defended the truth that Jesus is truly risen and that in being raised he is "the first fruit of those who have fallen asleep," Paul tackles the question of what it means to resurrected. "But someone will ask, 'How are the dead raised? With what kind of body do they come?' You foolish man!" It is foolish to ask such a question, for no comprehensible answer, at least at this point in *time*, is possible. Paul nonetheless provides what he hopes are helpful analogies. A grain of wheat is sown in one form of "body" and rises in another form. There are also many forms of "bodies"—human, animal, some have the bodies of birds or fish. "There are celestial bodies and there are terrestrial bodies; but the glory of the celestial is one, and the glory of the terrestrial is another."

> So is it with the resurrection of the dead. What is sown is per-
> ishable, what is raised is imperishable. It is sown in dishonor, it
> is raised in glory. It is sown in weakness, it is raised in power. It
> is sown a physical body, it is raised a spiritual body. If there is
> a physical body, there is also a spiritual body. Thus it is written,
> "The first man Adam became a living being"; the last Adam
> became a life-giving spirit. But it is not the spiritual which is
> first, but the physical, and then the spiritual. The first man was
> from the earth, a man of dust; the second man is from heaven.
> As was the man of dust, so are those who are of the dust; and
> as is the man of heaven, so are those who are in heaven. Just as
> we have borne the image of the man of dust, we shall also bear
> the image of the man of heaven. I tell you this, brethren: flesh
> and blood cannot inherit the kingdom of God, nor does the
> perishable inherit the imperishable.

For Paul, when the trumpet sounds on the last day, "the dead will be raised imperishable, and we shall be changed. For this per-ishable nature must put on the imperishable, and the mortal nature must put on immortality." When this comes to pass, death will no longer be victorious, and so it will lose its sting. "But thanks be to God, who gives us victory through our Lord Jesus Christ."[8]

First, Paul delineates a series of contrasting states of being— that of pre-resurrection feebleness and that of post-resurrection glory. These contrasts include both Jesus and those who share in his resurrection. In the resurrection, what was perishable becomes imperishable, what was dishonorable becomes glorious, what was

8. All of the above quotations are from 1 Cor 15.

weak is raised in power, and what was a physical body becomes a spiritual body. Second, the first of these contrasts are inherited from the first Adam, who was a living being. But he was from the dust of the earth, and his progeny bear his dust-born nature—even Jesus was a member of the sinful race of Adam. What comes second is the fruit of the last Adam—the risen Jesus, who is a life-giving spirit. Jesus is a life-giving spirit not in the sense that he is no longer a human being, but rather he is empowered, as gloriously risen, to breathe forth the Holy Spirit upon those who believe in him. As God breathed his life-giving spirit upon the first Adam, so Jesus now breathes forth his *risen* Spirit upon those who believe in him, thus making them new creations in him. Christians are no longer men composed of Adam's dust, but they are re-created men and women who partake of Jesus' risen, life-giving Spirit. They now bear his risen, heavenly image. In the above, it would appear that Paul is speaking of a transformation both in the sense of what takes place when a person becomes a Christian, which will be discussed shortly, and what takes place at the end of time—when the trumpet is blown. At the return of Jesus in glory, the dead, the perishable and mortal, will be raised and assume the fullness of imperishability and immortality. Death will be vanquished with its sting, and therefore Christians should thank God, who gives them victory through their risen Lord Jesus Christ.

Now, Paul realizes that what he has articulated concerning those attributes that are found within the last Adam, the risen Jesus, and which pertain to those who believe in him, are not fully comprehensible. They are linguistically negative attributes—nonperishable and non-mortal. We do not know, therefore, what it means to be imperishable and immortal, and the reason is that all of these attributes, in their primary and original meaning, pertain to the incomprehensible divine mode of being. They depict the manner in which the persons of the Trinity possess the attribute "eternity." Important nonetheless, Paul has ascribed these very divine attributes to the risen human Jesus and to those who share in his risen life. The risen Jesus and those who are in communion with him partake, in a human manner, of the divine attribute "eternity," for they become imperishable and immortal. They are assumed into the Trinity's divine glory and power—the divine mode of spiritual being. The faithful are taken up, in union with the ascended risen Jesus, into the heavenly realm—the kingdom of God. Thus while they live in time, they no longer solely live in the earthly realm of time—the realm of perishability, dishonor, weakness; the time-filled realm of the physical body composed of dust. They are no longer children of the first Adam, the first human being to experience time-measured change. Rather, Christians, as children of the last Adam, now live within the heavenly realm, within the very eternal life of the Trinity, and in so doing, they share the Trinity's eternal attributes—time is now deified, for it enters into the realm of the eternal. That deification of time is defined by employing the very incomprehensible attributes that apply to the Trinity's eternity—imperishability, immortality, and the like.

We have been articulating the new risen life that pertains to Christians who abide in the risen Christ, but how does this "abiding" come about? How is one made a new creation in Christ? How does one share in Jesus' risen glory and so take on the eternal attributes of imperishability and immortality? To these questions we now turn, for in answering them we discover how Christians in this life of time relate to the eternal life of the Trinity, a relationship that anticipates the fullness of eternal life.

CHAPTER SEVEN

Baptism & the Eucharist

Abiding in Christ

Introduction

Although Jesus, through his death and resurrection, sanctified history by obtaining the forgiveness of sin, the conquering of death, and the outpouring of the Holy Spirit, as we have seen, one must come to abide in him if one is to reap these salvific benefits. The sacraments are the efficacious signs through and in which Christians enter into the saving mysteries, the abiding in the crucified and risen Jesus, and so come to share the eternal life of the Trinity. Jesus' death and resurrection were therefore for the sake of the sacraments—particularly baptism and the Eucharist. Christians, in a human manner, come to possess the eternal divine attributes of imperishability and immortality. Here, in order to appreciate this new relationship between eternity and time, we examine baptism and the Eucharist.[1] We will first study John's Gospel and Paul's letters

---

1. I have chosen to focus on these two, not because the other sacraments are not important in this regard, but because in baptism we enter into the Christian life. This inauguration finds its culmination in the Eucharist.

concerning baptism, and then do the same with regards to their teaching on the Eucharist.

Baptism: The Deification of Time

In the Evangelist's Gospel, John the Baptist declares that although he baptizes with water, Jesus, the Father's Spirit-anointed Son of God, will "baptize with the Holy Spirit."[2] This baptism with the Holy Spirit is the fruit of Jesus' saving death and resurrection, for the Holy Spirit interiorly cleanses one of sin and makes one holy. Jesus himself informs Nicodemus that "unless one is born anew, he cannot see the kingdom of God." Only by being "born of water and the Holy Spirit" can one "enter the Kingdom of God," for what "is born of flesh is flesh" and what "is born of the Spirit is spirit."[3] Time-born flesh is of this world, the realm of sin and death, but one who is born of water and the Spirit is born into the kingdom of God, and so enters into the realm of eternal life. Ultimately, to abide in God's kingdom is to abide in the risen Jesus, for on the cross he put to death his time-born flesh, and in his resurrection he himself came to embody the fullness of the Spirit's eternal divine life.

Moreover, John's Gospel has multiple allusions to baptism, such as the healing of the man at the pool of Bethesda and the man born blind. Both miracles involved water, signifying rebirth and re-creation.[4] Likewise, Jesus' encounter with the Samaritan woman at Jacob's well alludes to baptism. He assures the woman that if she knew the gift of God and who it was who is speaking to her, she would have asked him, and he would have given her "living water." Unlike the water from Jacob's well, Jesus declares that "whoever

2. Jn 1:33–34.
3. Jn 3:3–6.
4. See Jn 5:2–11 and 9:1–41.

drinks of the water I shall give him will never thirst; the water that I shall give him will become in him a spring of water welling up to eternal life."[5] Later, Jesus declares: "If anyone thirsts, let him come to me and drink. He who believes in me, as the scripture has said, 'Out of his heart shall flow rivers of living water.'" In an aside, the Evangelists informs the reader: "Now this he said about the Spirit, which those who believed in him were to receive; for as yet the Spirit had not been given, because Jesus was not yet glorified."[6] Only after Jesus is glorified—that is, only after he is assumed into eternal life—is he empowered to give the living water that is the Holy Spirit, the Spirit that wells up to eternal life within the hearts of those who believe in him. The living water of the Holy Spirit must first, then, well up within the heart of the risen Jesus before he can pour it into the hearts of the faithful and so give them a share in eternal life.[7] Only by abiding within the Spirit-filled heart of the glorified and risen Jesus through baptism do Christians obtain eternal life. The emphasis throughout is on "eternal life"—the coming to live in communion with the Father through the indwelling Spirit by abiding in the risen Jesus, the Father's Spirit-filled, glorified incarnate Son. Thus, here on earth, Christians, having been born anew, already possess eternal life even though they still abide in time, and they do so in the expectancy of its eternal fulfillment.[8]

Now, Paul reminds his Roman readers that they are no longer

5. Jn 4:10–14.
6. Jn 7:37–39.
7. The phrase "out of his heart" can refer to Jesus' risen heart, to the heart of the believer, or to both. I believe, as seen above, that it refers to both—the Spirit-filled waters of eternal life flow from the heart of the risen Jesus and therefore well up within the hearts of those whom he baptizes with the Holy Spirit.
8. For a fuller theological understanding of baptism within John' Gospel, see my *Jesus Becoming Jesus: A Theological Interpretation of the Gospel of John, The Prologue and the Book of Signs*, vol. 2 (Washington, DC: Catholic University of America Press, 2021), 108–12, 129–44, 155–76, and 314–37.

to continue in sin. "Do you not know that all of us who have been baptized into Christ Jesus were baptized into his death? We were buried therefore with him by baptism into his death, so that as Christ was raised from the dead by the glory of the Father, we too might walk in newness of life."[9] For Paul, Jesus put to death our sinful flesh, our "old self," so that "our sinful body might be destroyed, and we might no longer be enslaved by sin."[10] In baptism, Christians efficaciously replicate, enact, Jesus' death, burial, and resurrection. "For if we have been united with him in a death like his, we shall certainly be united with him in his resurrection."[11] If we have died with Christ, we are assured of living with him.[12] Since Christ is raised from the dead, he will never die again, for "death no longer has dominion over him. The death he died he died to sin, once for all, but the life he lives he lives to God." The Romans must therefore consider themselves "dead to sin and alive to God in Christ Jesus."[13] Having been baptized into Christ, what characteristics accompany this new life in the Spirit? For the Romans, Paul provides the following enumeration.

First, those who are in Christ are freed from the condemnation of sin and death.[14] Second, Christians, because they no longer live by the flesh, are to set their minds on the things of the Spirit.[15]

9. Rom 6:1–4.

10. Rom 6:6. Paul tells the Corinthians that they must remember that "anyone in Christ, he is a new creation; the old has passed away, behold the new has come" (2 Cor 5:17).

11. Rom 6:5.

12. See Rom 6:8.

13. Rom 6:10–11.

14. See Rom 8:1–4.

15. See Rom 8:5–8. Paul reminds the Colossians that because they have been raised with Christ, they are to set their "minds on things that are above, not on things that are of earth." They have died, and now their "life is hidden with Christ in God." When Christ returns, they "will appear with him in glory" (Col 3:1–4).

Third, because Christians are "in the Spirit," they are assured that
the Spirit through whom the Father raised Jesus from the dead "will
give life to your moral bodies also through his Spirit who dwells in
you."[16] Fourth, "all who are led by the Spirit of God are sons of
God." Therefore they, in communion with Jesus, the Son, can cry
out, "Abba! Father!" In so doing, the Spirit is bearing witness that
we are children of God, "and if children, then heirs, heirs of God
and fellow heirs with Christ." If Christians suffer with Christ, they
will "also be glorified with him."[17] Fifth, thus, the sufferings in this
life "are not worth comparing with the glory that is to be revealed
to us."[18] Sixth, nonetheless, the whole of "creation waits with eager
longing for the revealing of the sons of God," for then "creation
itself will be set free from its bondage to decay and obtain the glorious liberty of the children of God." Until that *time*, the whole
of creation is "groaning in travail," and not only creation, "but we
ourselves who have the first fruits of the Spirit groan inwardly as
we wait for adoption as sons, the redemption of our bodies. For in
this hope we were saved."[19] Thus, for Christians, every successive
present human enactment of the future is an act of groaning in the
Spirit, an act that awaits in hope the final act wherein they will be
perfected. Moreover, although Christians continue to live in time,
the time that they presently experience already contains within it
an "eternal" quality. In the eternal Spirit, they already abide in the

16. Rom 8:9–11.

17. Rom 8:14–17. See also Gal 4:6–7. For Paul, the indwelling Holy Spirit is then
"the guarantee of our inheritance"—the glory of sharing in Jesus' immortal and
imperishable resurrected nature (Eph 1:14, see also 2 Cor 5:5).

18. Rom 8:18. Again, Paul makes a similar point in his Letter to the Corinthians. While in this world of time, they experience suffering, yet "this affliction
is preparing for us an eternal weight of glory beyond all comparison, because we
look not to the things that are seen but to the things that are unseen; for the things
that are seen are transient, but things that are unseen are eternal" (2 Cor 4:17–18).

19. Rom 8:19–24.

resurrected humanity of Jesus, the eternal Son, and so abide with the eternal Father as his children. Last, Paul assures the Romans that "those whom he [the Father] foreknew he also predestined to be conformed to the image of his Son, in order that he might be the first-born among many brethren. And those whom he predestined he also called; and those whom he called he also justified; and those whom he justified he also glorified."[20] For Paul, all those whom the Father eternally knew as his elect progress, within time, from first being called and to then being justified so as reach their eternal end—that of being glorified. In being glorified, they are conformed into the image of the Father's resurrected Son, thus making Jesus the firstborn of many brethren. For those who live in the risen Spirit-filled Jesus Christ, sanctified *time* possesses an *eternal* trajectory. Only those who live in the risen Christ can call God their Father both *now* and *forever*. Christians "are more than conquerors," for nothing, on earth or in heaven, can "separate us from the love of God in Christ Jesus our Lord."[21]

For Paul, the efficacious end of baptism is that one becomes a member of Christ's body. The risen Jesus Christ, as "the first born from the dead" is "the head of the body, the church," and all the baptized are conjoined members to his risen living and glorified body, for all share in the one divine life of the Holy Spirit.[22] "For just as the body is one and has many members, and all the members of the body, though many, are one body, so it is with Christ. For by one Spirit we were all baptized into one body—Jews or Greeks, slaves or free—and all were made to drink of one Spirit."[23] There is, then, "one body, one Spirit, ... one Lord, one faith, one baptism,

20. Rom 8:29–30.
21. Rom 8:37–39.
22. Col 1:18. See also Eph 1:22–23.
23. 1 Cor 12:12–13. See also Gal 3:28, Eph 2:13–13, and Col 3:11.

one God and Father of us all, who is above all and through all and in all."[24] Because there are many individual members within the one body of Christ, each member, as in a human body, is given a specific office or grace for the building up of the body of Christ, "until we are to attain to the unity of the faith and of the knowledge of the Son of God, to mature manhood, to the measure of the stature of the fullness of Christ."[25] Prior to reaching full maturity in Christ, we "are to grow up in every way into him who is the head, into Christ, from whom the whole body, joined and knit together by every joint with which it is supplied, when each part is working properly, makes bodily growth and upbuilds itself in love."[26] Thus Christ is creating "in himself one new man."[27] Moreover, the unity between Christ and his members, and the oneness of the members among themselves, is such that, as in a human body, all members of Christ's body suffer together, as do all members rejoice when one member is honored.[28]

As is evident from the above, the phrase "the body of Christ" is not merely a metaphor employed by Paul to accentuate the close unity between Christ and Christians. Rather, it is a metaphysical reality—Christ and his body, the church, form one living entity.

24. Eph 4–6.
25. Eph 4:11–13. See also Rom 12:4–8 and 1 Cor 12:27–30.
26. Eph 4:15–16.
27. Eph 2:15.
28. See 1 Cor 12:26 and Eph 4:25. When the risen Lord appeared in glory to Paul on the road to Damascus, he said to him, "Saul, Saul, why do you persecute me?" In response, Paul asked, "Who are you, Lord?" In turn, the Lord responded, "I am Jesus, whom you are persecuting" (Acts 9:3–5). In this interchange, Paul perceived two interrelated truths. Although he was persecuting Jesus' followers, he was actually persecuting Jesus himself, for his followers were members of his one body of which of he is the risen Lord. For a fully study of the theological significance of Paul's conversion experience, see my "Paul's Conversion in His Own Words," in *The Book of Acts: Catholic, Orthodox, and Evangelical Readings*, ed. Charles Raith II (Washington, DC: Catholic University of America Press, 2019), 175–87.

Now, the oneness of Christ and his body is unique in that it is composed of Christ, the head, and the members of the church—those who abide in him in heaven, those who are being purified in purgatory, and those who abide in him on earth.[29] What makes the one reality of Christ and his body unique is that it possesses, in a human manner, attributes that pertain to the eternity of the Trinity as well as attributes that pertain to the created order of time. All the members of Christ's body, whether in heaven, in purgatory, or on earth, share to various degrees in the risen glory of their risen head, the Lord Jesus Christ. Being conjoined to the risen humanity of the incarnate Son of God, through the shared indwelling of the one Holy Spirit, they abide in communion with the Father as his children. Thus all members of Christ's body, again to various degrees, abide within the divine life of the Trinity and therefore share in its immortal and imperishable nature. In so doing, they also partake of all other divine attributes, such as the Trinity's divine knowledge, wisdom, power, and love. For those on earth, then, while they live within the ever-changing reality of time, they simultaneously live within the heavenly realm of eternity, for they are one with their risen Lord Jesus Christ. They share already in Jesus' risen immortal and imperishable nature as Spirit-transformed adopted children of the Father.

What is also unique concerning the relationship between Christ and his body is that while Jesus, as bodily risen, is fully and perfectly glorified, he nonetheless undergoes change in relation to

29. Significantly, the body of Christ is composed of not only those who live on earth, but also those who have died—those in purgatory and the saints in heaven. This being the case, those on earth can pray on behalf of the those in purgatory, and they can request that the saints intercede on their own behalf. Being members of the one body of Christ, the saints in heaven are lovingly solicitous for their brothers and sisters on earth. Being in communion with one another, all members of the body of Christ are in a living relationship with one another.

those members who still abide in time. As the members of Christ's body assume the attributes ascribed to eternity, so Christ, as head of his body, assumes the attributes ascribed to time. As Paul notes, when members of his body suffer, the risen Jesus himself, as the head of his body, suffers, as do all the other members of his body. When members of his body are honored, Jesus himself, as head of his body, is honored, as are all the other members of his body. The reason that the risen Jesus undergoes change is because the earthly members of his body still abide in the changing realm of time. Thus, although Jesus, as the divine Son of the Father, is unchangeable, for he possesses the attribute of eternity, because of his oneness with those who are united to him, he undergoes change within his risen human mode of existence.[30]

Because of this unity of eternity and time within the body of Christ, the oneness between Christ and his body, the Catholic Church has traditionally employed the term "Mystical Body of Christ." The word "body" acknowledges that the body of Christ is composed of both Jesus' human risen material body and the material bodies of its members, and therefore there resides the element of time within the body of Christ—at least until Jesus returns in glory.[31] The term "mystical" accentuates the divine, eternal aspect of the body of Christ—the heavenly characteristic wherein Jesus, the risen incarnate Son of God, and his members are assumed into the eternal life of the Trinity. What conjoins the "mystical" and the "bodily" is the Holy Spirit, for, in baptism, it is he who transforms the earthly baptized into the likeness of the risen Jesus, the Father's Son, and so fashions them into children of the

30. For a further exposition of Christ suffering in union with the members of his body, see my *Does God Suffer?*, 243–59.

31. I later discuss whether there will be "time" after Jesus comes at the "end of time."

Father. The Holy Spirit can thus be considered the soul of the Mystical Body of Christ, for he constitutes the living oneness between Christ and the members of his body.[32]

Here, we again perceive the difference between the old Mosaic Passover covenant and the new and everlasting Passover covenant established in Jesus. Although God in the old covenant established a unique relationship with the Israelites, they were not interiorly transformed, thus rendering them incapable of keeping the covenant. Through his death and resurrection, however, Jesus, as the incarnate Father's Son, established a covenant wherein those who abide in the risen Jesus are transformed into his likeness. Sharing in the likeness of Christ, empowered by the indwelling Holy Spirit, Christians are rendered capable of living holy lives, for they have become new creations in Christ. Precisely because they no longer exist solely in the realm of time, within time they are able to live in a heavenly manner, a holy way of life that befits their being in communion with the risen Jesus. Christians, then, are to heed Paul's exhortations. Having been set free of the sins of the flesh, Christians are "to walk by the Spirit" and so bear the fruit of the Spirit: "love, joy, peace, patience, kindness, goodness, faithfulness, gentleness, and self-control."[33] Such fruit of the Spirit testifies that Christians already partake in a human manner of the holy attributes that comprise the Trinity's eternal manner of existence.

---

32. The *Catechism of the Catholic Church*, §797, states:

"What the soul is to the human body, the Holy Spirit is to the Body of Christ, which is the Church" [St. Augustine, *Sermo*, 267]. "To this Spirit of Chris, as an invisible principle, is to be ascribed the fact that all the parts of the body are joined one with the other and with their exalted head; for the whole Spirit of Christ is in the head, the whole Spirit is in the body, and the whole Spirit is in each of the members" [Pius XII, encyclicaly, *Mystici Corporis*].

33. Gal 5:18–25. See also Eph 4:17–32.

The Eucharist: Abiding in Time and in Eternity

Having examined baptism as found within John's Gospel and Paul's Letters, we can turn to the topic of the Eucharist. Although the Evangelist does not narrate the institution of the Eucharist within his account of the Last Supper, he does provide Jesus' lengthy Eucharistic discourse in chapter 6 of his Gospel. Jesus' multiplication of the loaves and fish is the prelude to this discourse—the only miracle contained in all four Gospels. Within the Synoptic accounts, Jesus' words and actions, when multiplying the loaves and fish, more fully anticipate the words he will use and the actions he will enact when instituting the Eucharist at the Last Supper. Nonetheless, all accounts portray the miraculous multiplication as a prophetic sign of the Eucharist—the abundance of life signified in the twelve remaining baskets of bread.[34]

Jesus tells the crowd who sought him subsequent to the multiplication that they have done so "not because you saw signs, but because you ate your fill of the loaves. Do not labor for the food that perishes, but for the food which endures to eternal life, which the Son of man will give you; for on him God the Father set his seal."[35] Note the contrast between the food that "perishes" and the food that endures to "eternal life." The food of this present world of time "perishes," as do those who eat it. But the food that Jesus,

---

34. For a more detailed theological interpretation of the miracle of the loaves and fish, as well as its relations to the Synoptic and Johannine accounts of the Eucharist, see my *Jesus Becoming Jesus: A Theological Interpretation of the Synoptic Gospels* (Washington, DC: Catholic University of American Press, 2018), 133–39 and 297–313, and *Jesus Becoming Jesus: A Theological Interpretation of the Gospel of John: The Prologue and the Book of Signs*, vol. 2 (Washington, DC: Catholic University of America Press, 2021, 215–57).

35. All the following quotations will be from Jn 6 unless otherwise noted.

the Son of man whom the Father has sealed in the Holy Spirit, will give endures unto eternal life. It does not belong to the perishable world of time. The crowd asks for a sign by which they could come to believe in him. They offer, as an example, their ancestors having eaten manna in the desert—the miraculous bread that God gave them from heaven. Ironically, Jesus has just previously performed that very sign, a sign that they did not grasp in their blind pursuit of perishable food. Jesus reminds them that it was not Moses who gave them bread from heaven, but his Father. "For the bread of God is that which comes down from heaven, and gives life to the world." In response, the people request that Jesus always give them such bread. Jesus, in turn, declares: "I am (*ego eimi*) the bread of life." Jesus is the bread of life because he is the divine Son of God, He Who Is, who has come down from heaven in becoming man. Jesus, the Son, has come to do the work of his Father. "For this is the will of my Father, that everyone who sees the Son and believes in him should have eternal life; and I will raise him up at the last day." Some were displeased that Jesus said, "I am the bread which came down from heaven." They note that Jesus is the son of Joseph, whom they know along with his mother. That Jesus is the bread of life depends, then, upon who is Jesus' father. If Joseph is his father, then he is not the bread that comes down from heaven. If God is his Father, then the man Jesus is the Father's Son, and so the bread that has come down from heaven. Jesus declares that he is the latter. "I am the living bread which came down from heaven; if anyone eats this bread, he will live forever; and the bread which I will give for the life of the world is my flesh."

Thus far, Jesus' Eucharistic discourse, with his responses to the skeptical crowd, primarily focuses upon the Incarnation. Who is the earthly man Jesus? Is he God's Son? Who is his true Father? As stated previously, the Incarnation is the incomparable mystery wherein eternity and time are united. They become one in the person of the incarnate Son. Only if Jesus is the Father's Son, the Son of the eternal life-giving Father, could he be the life-giving bread that has come down from heaven. Only if he is the earthly incarnate He Who Is can he be the heavenly given bread of eternal life. As also previously seen, however, the Incarnation is the necessary prelude to the further salvific work that Jesus needs enact. He must give his flesh for the life of the world and that "giving" is first the "giving" of his life to his Father as the perfect Passover sacrifice with its resulting glorious resurrection. Only as the risen incarnate Son of the Father can Jesus then give his risen flesh for the life of the world, for only the risen humanity of the divine Son bears within it eternal life. In the resurrection, Jesus' flesh becomes the living and life-giving bread that comes down from heaven—the bread that endures to eternal life. Upon this truth Jesus now expounds.

Again, in response to Jesus' declaration that it is his flesh that is the bread of life, the Jews disputed among themselves as to how this man could give them his flesh to eat. Jesus does not directly address their concern. Rather, he emphatically declares: "Truly, truly, I say to you, unless you eat the flesh of the Son of man and drink his blood, you have no life in you; he who eats my flesh and drinks my blood has eternal life, and I will raise him up at the last day." Jesus states that he who eats his flesh and drinks his blood "abides in me, and I in him. As the living Father sent me, and I live because of the Father, so he who eats me will live because of me. This is the bread which came down from heaven, not such as the fathers ate and died; he who eats this bread will live forever."

Jesus here speaks not only of eating his body, but also of drinking his blood. This twofold eating and drinking designates the sacrificial nature of the Eucharist. It is Jesus' given-up body and poured-out blood that is to be eaten and drunk, for only in lovingly offering himself to the Father on behalf of humankind is the sin and death of this perishable world vanquished. Moreover, in this sacrificial offering of himself, Jesus merits his resurrection. Thus the flesh that is to be eaten and the blood that is to be drunk is the now-risen-given-up flesh and the risen-given-up blood—the entirety of the Son's risen human self. By eating and drinking the crucified and now-risen Jesus, the faithful are conjoined to his once for all covenantal Passover sacrifice, and so, having been cleansed of sin, they are able to become one in him—they in him and he in them. By abiding in Jesus, they partake of his risen eternal life. As Jesus has eternal life from his Father as the Father's divine Son and presently shares in that eternal life as gloriously risen, so those who eat him will live because of him. They too will live forever. Thus to be in communion with the risen Jesus is to be in communion with his Father—the eternal fount of eternal life.

Importantly, to actually abide in the risen Jesus by partaking of his risen body and blood demands that the bread and wine of the Eucharist actually *become* and *be* the risen-given-up-body and the risen-given-up-blood. There must be change of "what-ness." What was once bread and wine must *become* and *be* Jesus himself. What must be eaten and drunk is Jesus, as he presently exists in the fullness of his resurrected glory. If the Eucharist is not actually the risen Jesus, then he is not actually the living bread that comes down from heaven. Likewise, if one is not in actual communion with the risen Jesus, in a real abiding oneness, then one will not share in and so partake of eternal life, for the risen Jesus literally embodies eternal life. In the Eucharist, the faithful embody here on earth, because they abide in Jesus, his eternal life, and so ascend in him into the heavenly realm. Thus, again, they embody, while living in time, the divine attributes that pertain to eternity—imperishability and immortality. What is eaten here on earth is, then, a foretaste of what will be fulfilled when Jesus raises up on the last day all who have abided in him while on earth. Therefore the manna that God gave the Israelites in the desert prophetically anticipates both the Incarnation, the Son of God coming down from heaven and coming to exist as man, as well as the Eucharist, the risen incarnate Son of God coming down from heaven as the true bread of everlasting life.

Within John's Gospel, baptism and the Eucharist are consecutively conjoined. In inaugurating his Father's salvific work, this sequential conjoining is perceived and anticipated in Jesus' first sign, that of changing water into wine. The twelve water-filled jars signify the abundance of life given in baptism. In the ushering of this water to the steward, it becomes wine—the sign of the fullness of life that is found in the Eucharist. Thus those who come to believe that Jesus is the Father's Son first partake of baptism, wherein by the power of the Holy Spirit they are born anew in him. Upon receiving this sacrament, they are ushered into full communion with him by eating and drinking his risen body and blood. This first anticipatory sign finds its fulfillment upon the cross.

Jesus declares: "It is finished." Having completed his Father's saving work, Jesus immediately "bowed his head and gave up his spirit."[36] Death did not overcome him; rather, Jesus actively completed his Father's work in the conjoined act of giving up his spirit unto his Father, which simultaneously empowered him to breathe fourth his Spirit upon the church, the fruit of the priestly offering of himself to his Father as the perfect all-holy sacrifice. Now, in his breathing forth of his Spirit, Jesus effected the means by which those who believe in him might participate in his saving

36. Jn 19:30.

mysteries—his death and resurrection. These saving means are the sacraments of baptism and the Eucharist, for from Jesus' pieced side "came out blood and water."[37] To partake of the fruit of the cross, the tree of life, is to partake of baptism and the Eucharist. In the Spirit-filled waters of baptism the Christian is born anew into the crucified and risen Christ, and in the Eucharist the Christian is then subsumed into communion with the crucified and risen Lord himself—the eating of his risen-offered-up body and the drinking of his risen-poured-out blood. Thus what first prophetically began at Cana finds it completion on the cross—the instituting of baptism and the Eucharist. Moreover, as the crucified Jesus passed over from death to life, so Christians, by means of baptism and the Eucharist, also pass over—in, with, and through Christ— from the time-bound world of sin and death into the Father's realm of eternal life.

As found in his First Letter to the Corinthians, Paul's understanding of the Eucharist is less developed than found in John's Gospel, though it is no less profound. The difference lies in that Paul articulated his understanding of the Eucharist within the context of particular abuses within the Corinthian community—"because when you come together it is not for the better but for the worse."[38] Paul's concern is that when the Corinthians "assemble as a church (ekklesia), I hear that there are divisions among you." Because of the factions, "it is not the Lord's supper that you eat." These divisions arise within the meal that is eaten prior to the Eucharist itself. Each faction (apparently one is rich and other poor) eats its own meal, wherein one group goes hungry and the other gets drunk. Such meals, Paul reminds the rich, could be eaten in

37. Jn 19:34.
38. 1 Cor 11:17. All the following quotations are from 1 Cor 11:17–34 unless otherwise noted.

their respective houses. "Or do you despise the church (*ekklesias*) of God and humiliate those who have nothing." Such behavior cannot be commended. Paul then professes what he has received from the Lord and will now deliver to them.

On the night when he was betrayed, Jesus took bread, and giving thanks, he blessed and broke it saying: "This is my body which is for you. Do this in remembrance of me." Likewise, he took the cup, saying: "This cup is the new covenant in my blood. Do this, as often as you drink it, in remembrance of me."

In doing what Jesus commanded, the Corinthians "proclaim the Lord's death until he comes." Because the Eucharistic bread and wine are the new covenantal sacrificial body and blood of the risen Lord, to partake of them unworthily is to profane "the body and blood of the Lord." Therefore the Corinthians must examine themselves, for "anyone who eats and drinks without discerning the body, eats and drinks judgment upon himself." Significantly, the Corinthians recognize neither that the bread is truly the body and blood of the risen Jesus nor that they themselves are the one body of Christ.[39] Because of this lack of discernment, many of the Corinthians are sick, and some have even died. Now, similar to what is found in John's Gospel, the Corinthians are first members of the one body of Christ because they are baptized into Christ. Having become members of the body of Christ, they are then able to share in the Eucharistic banquet, wherein the risen Jesus is truly present. By eating and drinking the risen body and blood of Jesus, the Corinthians become, through baptism, who they truly are—the

39. Here, scholars perceive that Paul is employing the term "body" both in the sense of Jesus' Eucharistic body as well as the members of his body. The Corinthians fail to acknowledge both that Christ's risen body is truly present and that they are members of Christ's body and so one in him.

one body of Christ. But the manner in which they are presently celebrating the Eucharist testifies that they recognize neither of these realities.

Now, in their lack of discernment, the Corinthians failed to recognize that although it is an event enacted in time on earth, the Eucharist is founded upon and enacted in a manner that transcends time, for, as the baptized members of Christ's body, they are now partaking of the risen Jesus himself and so are together as one taken up in the heavenly divine realm that transcends the earthly realm of time. They failed to discern the "eternality" of the Eucharistic event they celebrated—that together they are being subsumed into the risen Spirit-filled Christ wherein they themselves, in communion with Christ, enter into the very presence of their timeless Father. The Eucharist is the present fullest deification of time here on earth and so anticipates time's complete deification, when the one body of Christ will share fully in Jesus' risen humanity as the Father's children.

CHAPTER EIGHT

Relational Sacramentality

The Metaphysics and Epistemology of Eternity and Time

Introduction

In the above examination of baptism and the Eucharist, I have purposely employed and solely commented upon scriptural concepts and language. But the biblical concepts and language, as found in John's Gospel and Paul's Letters, contain within them a sacramental metaphysics and epistemology that is relational in nature. The sacramental actions, while enacted on earth, conjoin time with what transcends time, that is, the risen Jesus. Being conjoined to the risen Jesus, moreover, time enters into the realm of the eternal—the very manner in which the Trinity exists in itself. Within these singular sacramental metaphysical relationships there is also a unique manner of knowing, both on the part of the persons of the Trinity and on the part of human beings.

To grasp the metaphysical relationships contained within the sacraments, we need to review the various types of relationships that can be established. First, we saw that the persons of the Trinity are "real" relationships among themselves, for they are only who they are as subsistent-relations-fully-in-act only in relation to one another. Their relationships constitute their eternal identities as Father, Son, and Holy Spirit. Second, through the divine act of creation, a "mixed" relationship is established between God or the Trinity and the created order. The relationship on the part of the creature is "real" in that it comes to be. Although the relationship on the part of the Trinity is termed "unreal" in that the Trinity does not change in enacting the act of creation, it is "actually" related to the creature, for the creature is "really" related to the Trinity as the Trinity actually immutably exists in itself. Likewise, the incarnational relationship is also a "mixed" relation. The humanity is "really" related to the Son, for it comes to be and is ontologically united to the Son as the Son exists. Although the relationship on the part of the Son is said be "unreal" in that the Son does not change in the act of the incarnational "becoming," the Son is "actually" related to the humanity, for the humanity is "really" related to the Son as the Son immutably exists in himself. Therefore the Son actually exists as an authentic man. With the above in mind, the question arises as to what kind of relationship exists between the resurrected incarnate Son of God, Jesus, and with those who are sacramentally united to him, and thus the kind of relationship that exists between Christ and his body. Moreover, in being related to the risen Jesus, what kind of relationship exists between the Christian and the Trinity? The metaphysical nature of these relationships will determine the manner in which Christians know the Trinity and the Trinity knows Christians. Ultimately, then, these sacramental relationships will determine the type of relationship that exists between eternity and time, and so the manner in which Christians know the persons of the Trinity and the persons of the Trinity know them.

A Real Relationship: Christ and His Body

Now, although the Creator/creature relationship is a mixed relationship, the relationship between the risen Jesus and the Christian, as a member of his body, is a "real" relationship, in that both the risen Jesus and the Christian are changed in the act by which the relationship is established. By being baptized into Christ, the Christian is born anew into Christ through the transforming power of the Holy Spirit. The Christian is thus changed from being a sinner, with its curse of death, into being a child of the Father by abiding in Christ the Son, and thus an inheritor of eternal life.[1] Reciprocally, Jesus, as head of his body, is changed, for he is now the Lord and Savior of a newly conjoined member. Moreover, the entire body of Christ is changed, for a new member has been incorporated into it. Thus, metaphysically, the intimacy of this saving relationship differs in kind from that of the Creator/creature relationship, for timebound human beings are now subsumed into the eternal life of the Trinity, wherein they acquire, in a human manner, the divine attributes of immortality and incorruptibility. Metaphysically, time is assumed into eternity, for those who live in time have been deified—share in the eternal divine life of the Trinity itself. What must be accentuated here is the risen *humanity* of the divine Son. The risen *humanity* of the divine Son makes it

---

1. Christians do continue to sin, but they now do so within the context of being saved, of being re-created in Christ. Thus, in acknowledging their sin and asking forgiveness, they continue in their growth in holiness through Jesus' reciprocal act of forgiveness.

possible for a "real" reciprocal relationship to be established between the Son and human beings. Apart from the risen humanity, no "real" abiding relationship could be established between the divine Son and human beings. Here, the Eucharist finds its supreme importance.

In the Eucharist the "real" relationship that was first established between Christ and his body in baptism finds it summit, for the members of his body here on earth come into communion with Jesus as he himself now exists as risen. Christians eat his risen-given-up body and drink his risen-poured-out blood. Because the risen Jesus himself is "really" present in the Eucharistic, he and his earthly members "really" become one. Their "real" relationship is enacted as fully as possible here on earth, for Christians "really" abide in the risen Jesus, and the risen Jesus "really" abides in them. Within this mutual Eucharistic abiding, Christians share in Jesus' risen incorruptibility and immortality—attributes that pertain to divine eternity.[2]

Moreover, the "real" baptismal and Eucharistic relationships between the risen Jesus and Christians are therefore not static but grow and mature over the course of time. As members are added to Christ's body, and as the body is strengthened through the various ministries and gifts among its members throughout the ages, Jesus extends his salvific lordship, and his body increases in holiness. The metaphysical relational bonding of Christ and his body, the becoming ever more one through the life and love of the Holy Spir-

2. Here we perceive the importance of the Catholic understanding of the nature of Christ's presence in the Eucharist—that of transubstantiation. Only if the bread and wine are actually changed into the body and blood of Jesus, the risen Jesus, are Christians able to be in communion with Jesus as Jesus is in his risen state. By being united to Jesus as he exists in his risen state, earthly Christians are taken up, in, with, and through Christ, into the eternal life of the Trinity, and so humanly share in their incorruptible and immortal nature.

it, advances and evolves. Such is the meaning of Paul's declaration: "And we all, with unveiled face, beholding the glory of the Lord, are being changed into his likeness from one degree of glory to another; for this comes from the Lord who is the Spirit."[3] The closer this relational bond increases between Christians, who are members of his body, and the risen Lord Jesus, the more they assume here on earth the resurrected life of Jesus, and so obtain, ever more fully, the divine attribute of eternal glory—the life of the Trinity itself.

Such an understanding is in keeping with what Paul prays on behalf the Ephesians. He prays to his Father, the source of all fatherhood, that the Ephesians, "according to the riches of his glory," might be interiorly strengthened through the Holy Spirit, so that Christ may dwell in them. Thus being "rooted and grounded in love," they "may have power to comprehend with all the saints what is the breadth and length and height and depth, and to know the love of Christ which surpasses knowledge, that you may be filled with all the fullness of God."[4] The riches of the Father's glory entail the progress of knowing the unfathomable love of Christ, a love that is incomprehensible. The more that Christians, as members of his body, grow in their communion with Christ through the Holy Spirit, the more they will come to know the depths of Christ's love—a love that defines the very fullness of God. Again, we perceive, in this growth in glory founded upon love, that earthly Christians are ever more subsumed into the eternal realm—even to the extent of being filled with the fullness of divine eternal life. Thus, for Christians, time is but the trajectory into eternity, for earthly time is becoming ever more deified. Within this trajectory, the ever-increasing metaphysical bonding with Christ in the love of the Spirit, there is also an epistemological growth—the ever-

3. 2 Cor 3:18.
4. Eph 3:14–19.

increasing knowledge of the incomprehensible love of Christ, a love that leads to the fullness of divine life. Paul notes that here on earth our knowledge is imperfect, but "when the perfect comes, the imperfect will pass away." The reason is that in time, "we see as in a mirror dimly, but then face to face. Now I know in part; then I shall understand fully, even as I have been fully understood."[5] In this life we know the mysteries of faith, but only imperfectly and dimly. When Christians obtain their risen perfection, while the divine mysteries will remain incomprehensible, they will know them perfectly, for they will see them face-to-face, that is, the mystery of the incarnate glorified Christ and, in him, the mystery of the Trinity itself. Thus, for Paul, quoting Isaiah, "no eye has seen, nor ear heard, nor the heart of man conceive, what God has prepared for those who love him."[6]

The Eschatological Relationship: The Full Deification of Time

Of course, as seen above, this metaphysical and epistemological trajectory only comes to completion when Jesus returns in glory at the end of time, for only then do those who have died in Christ come to share fully in his bodily resurrection. Again, the terminus of salvation, in accordance with the Father's divine plan, is that, in the fullness of *time*, all things are to be united in Christ, both on earth and in heaven.[7] Then the members of his body will fully

5. 1 Cor 13:9–12.

6. 1 Cor 2:9. Obviously, for the individual Christian, this growth from glory to glory can be interrupted or even terminated through mortal sin. Moreover, as is evident throughout history, the Church goes through periods of decline and renewal. Nonetheless, in the midst of these individual and historical cycles, the church continues to grow in holiness.

7. See Eph 1:9–10.

become new creations in Christ and thus possess a vision of God's incomprehensible being. Christ will then fully "create in himself one new man."[8] As one new man in Christ, Christians will "attain to the unity of the faith and of the knowledge of the Son of God, to mature manhood, of the measure of the stature of fullness of Christ."[9] For Paul, when the end comes and all of Christ's enemies are made subject to him, the last enemy being death itself, then the Son himself will also be subjected to him [his Father] who will put all things under him, "that God may be everything to everyone."[10] All that is united in Christ while here on timebound earth will, in him, become one in the very being of God. As quoted previously, when the trumpet sounds, "the dead will be raised imperishable, and we will be changed. For this perishable nature must put on the imperishable, and the mortal nature must put on immortality."[11] To be imperishable and immortal is to acquire, in a human manner, God's eternity.

In his First Letter, John expresses thoughts similar to those of Paul. He assures his beloved that "we are God's children now; it does not yet appear what we shall be, but we know that we will be like him, for we shall see him as he is."[12] Here in time, we are already God's children, for we abide in his risen Son, Jesus Christ. Nonetheless, we do not know what it will be like to achieve the fullness of the present reality. What we do know presently is that we will become like God himself, for already we are his adopted children in Christ the Son. The reason for this assurance is that we will see God as God is in himself. The question arises as to why we

8. Eph 2:15.
9. Eph 4:13.
10. 1 Cor 15:23–28.
11. 1 Cor 15:52–53.
12. 1 Jn 3:2.

will become like God because we see him. Why does seeing God make us like him, that is, sharing in his eternal divine life?

John, as far as we know, was not a "professional" philosopher, yet his declaration contains within it a realistic epistemology, one that would be in accord with Aristotle and Aquinas. Within a realistic epistemology, the knower, in coming to know, mentally comes to be the object known. For example, when someone sees a tree, that person first possesses, through his or her eyes, a physical image of the tree. Following upon this image, the intellect abstracts the essence, the "tree-ness," of the object seen, and in so doing, his or her intellect becomes the seen object. In seeing God as God is, the saints in heaven possess a vision of God wherein they are transformed into the very likeness of eternal God. They assume the eternality of God himself—his manner of being. Traditionally, this vision is termed beatific in that it is the vision of those beatified—the divine vision is itself the transforming beatification of the heavenly saints. Nonetheless, while the saints possess a transfiguring vision of God as God is, God continues to remain incomprehensible, for the very reason that what is beheld is the very mystery of God himself—the more God is known, the more incomprehensible he becomes.

Now, I am not entirely happy with the traditional understanding of what is termed "the beatific vision," for it does not, I believe, do justice to John's declaration.[13] The term "beatific vision" gives the impression that the beatified come to know fully an object over against or apart from themselves, that is, God, and so come to be divine like. Within the Johannine declaration, the faithful are already children of God. By abiding in the risen Jesus, the Son, they

13. See my full argumentation on this point, "Jesus' Filial Vision of the Father," in *Jesus: Essays in Christology* (Ave Maria, FL: Sapienta Press, 2014), 279–92, and "Thomas Joseph White's Beatific Vision of the Incarnate Son: A Response," in *Jesus: Essays in Christology*, 293–301.

are children of the Father through the transforming power of the Holy Spirit. Thus to see God face-to-face means that the faithful do so in union with the Spirit-filled Jesus, the Son, and so share in his own complete risen *filial vision* of his Father. The risen faithful do not behold something that is over against them. Rather, they fully behold the divine reality in which they already abide. As children of the Father who abide in his Son, they share in the risen Son's vision. They see God their Father face-to-face through the eyes of Jesus. The transfiguring epistemological realism of the saints is founded upon the transforming epistemological realism of the risen incarnate Son, for it is that risen filial vision that they share in communion with him. This interpretation of the Evangelist's declaration is both more Trinitarian as well as more in accord with Christians being members of Christ's body, both on earth and in heaven, and so partake of the heavenly vision that their head, Jesus, himself possesses.[14]

14. Two recent articles are relevant to the above discussion. This first is Neil Ormerod's "'And We Shall See Him Face to Face': A Trinitarian Analysis of the Beatific Vision," *Theological Studies* 82, no. 4 (2021): 646–62, and the second is Will Bankston's "Seeing God's Essence: A Teleological Coordination of the Beatific Vision and Christ's Work of Atonement," *Pro Ecclesia* 30, no. 4 (2021): 539–66. Although Ormerod addresses the nature of the "beatific vision" from the perspective "of what is generally called the 'interim state'—that is, the state of the blessed prior to the general resurrection," what he has to say pertains to my understanding (648). The purpose of his article is to provide a Trinitarian understanding of this heavenly vision. Following Bernard Lonergan, he argues that the beatific vision should be "correlated with the relation of filiation, whose term is the Father" (658). Thus the blessed in heaven possess a vision of the Father analogous to the Son's vision of the Father within the communion of the love of the Holy Spirit—"through participation in the filial relation, the blessed return to the Father as sons and daughters of God" (659). While the tradition "focused on the soul's vision of the divine essence," Ormerod argues that his understanding rightly focuses on a Trinitarian notion of the divine relations, relationships into which the blessed presently partake (661).

I am obviously sympathetic to Ormerod's proposal. The problem is that although he wants the heavenly vision of the blessed to be a filial vision, he fails to grasp fully that such a filial vision is only possible by abiding within the resurrected Jesus, and so share, within that abiding, his filial vision of the Father in communion with the love of the Holy Spirit. It would seem that Ormerod's understanding posits a filial vision, analogous to the Son, but one that is not obtained by abiding in the risen humanity of the Son, Jesus. Our entrance into the divine life of the Trinity, and so into their divine vision, is by being conjoined to the risen humanity of the Son, Jesus, wherein we partake of his Spirit-filled vision of his Father as the Father's children. See also Neil Ormerod and Christiaan Jacobs-Vandegeer, "Sacred Heart, Beatific Mind: Exploring the Consciousness of Jesus," *Theological Studies* 79, no. 4 (2018): 727–44.

I have similar concerns with Bankston's article. He is responding to recent books by Hans Boersma, *Seeing God: The Beatific Vision in Christian Tradition* (Grand Rapids, MI: Eerdmans, 2018), and Michael Allen, *Grounded in Heaven: Recentering Christian Hope and Life on God* (Grand Rapids, MI: Eerdmans, 2018). Both authors posit, in various ways, "the Incarnate Son as the direct object of the vision." Bankston, in contrast, argues that while the incarnate Son is necessary for the beatific vision, the vision itself is not of the incarnate Son but "the divine essence as the vision's direct object" (541). Which, then, is more theologically accurate—"gazing directly upon the divine essence or upon Christ" (541)?

Both Boersma and Allen argue, in differing manners, that it is in beholding the incarnate Son that one beholds the divine Son, and so in beholding the Son's divinity, one comes to behold the Father and the Holy Spirit as well (see 546–49). Bankston concludes, "Taken together, both Boersma and Allen affirm Christ as the direct object of the beatific vision.... Each has recourse to the hypostatic union as a means of equating our vision of Christ with our vision of God" (550).

Although Bankston affirms the importance of the Incarnation, he believes it is insufficient on its own to found a proper understanding of the beatific vision. He proposes that Incarnation was for the sake of the atonement and that the atonement was for the sake of the beatific vision. Thus the atonement restores humankind from sin and so restores its *telos*, that is, the vision of God. The risen humanity of the Son fulfills humankind's end, for the incarnate Son possesses a full vision of God (see 555). Thus, as the resurrected Christ beholds God's essence, so "it seems that one does better to hold that the direct object of the beatific vision is the very essence of God" (562). Since Christ has fulfilled humankinds eschatological end, the heavenly saints, those who partake of Christ saving work, come to enjoy a vision similar to his. While Bankston speaks of the faithful being members of Christ's body, it is by beholding the risen humanity of the incarnate Son that one has a vision of the divine essence. Bankston appears to hold that Christ's risen humanity mediates the vision of God's essence (see 563–64).

The problem I have with all three of the above authors is that they have made the incarnate Son an object to behold. In beholding the risen Jesus himself, one obtains the beatific vision (Boersma and Allen), or one beholds in beholding the risen Jesus the divine essence (Bankston). Either way, it seems to me, the direct intimacy of knowledge and love is absent within such an understanding of the beatific vision. Yes, both the Incarnation and atonement are necessary. As I have offered above, however, it is through faith and sacraments, particularly baptism and the Eucharist, that one is incorporated into the one reality that is the body of Christ—one comes to abide in Christ. By abiding in the risen Christ, one comes to abide within the Trinity as children of the Father by the transforming power of the Holy Spirit. Thus, at the end of time, one will come to share fully in Jesus' own filial vision of the Father in the love of the Holy Spirit. The beatific vision is not, then, the beholding of that which we are not in communion with, but rather, because we are in communion with the risen humanity of Christ the Son, we behold, as Spirit-filled children of the Father, that wherein we reside—the Trinity itself. The key truths here, truths that are absent in the above misconceptions, are that of *abiding in Christ* and so sharing in his *filial vision*.

CHAPTER NINE

Earthly & Heavenly Presentiality

Introduction

I have been emphasizing the mutually real relationship that exists between Christians, as members of Christ's body, with Jesus himself as the head of his body. I have noted the changes that take place within such a real relationship. The members of Christ's body experience not only changes within the realm of earthly time, but also ultimately in the final transforming change that takes place at the end of time—their final Spirit transfiguration into the full likeness of Jesus, the Son, so as to become perfect images of the Father as the Father's children. At this juncture, what is yet to be examined is the nature of the relationship between the risen incarnate Jesus with his heavenly Father, which would also, in turn, include the relationship of Christ's body with the Father. While the resurrection brings about a real change in Jesus and his relationship to his Father, does such a relationship also reciprocally bring about a change in his Father? Equally, while Christians are changed when becoming members of and living within Christ's body, and in their own resurrection at the end of time, does such a change in the faithful effect a corresponding change in God—the eternal Father, Son, and Holy Spirit? Again, we must examine the kind of relationship that is enacted. How is the risen Jesus present to his Father and his Father to him, and how are Christians, on earth and in heaven, present to the persons of the Trinity and the Trinity present to them?

Presentiality: A Mixed Relation

To address this issue, we must return to my understanding of Aquinas's notion of presentiality (*praesentialitate*). As we saw, when addressing God's knowledge of created reality, including future contingents, Aquinas states that God eternally knows all things as they are "in their presentiality (*praesentialitate*)."[1] This presentiality is founded upon the act of creation, which establishes a mixed relation. Within this relationship, although the Trinity does not change, it is *actually* related to the creature, for the creature is *really* related to it. Moreover, then, as the creature continuously enacts the future, and so its potentiality, it is ever, within the flow of time, newly related to the Trinity as the Trinity is, and so the Trinity is ever present to the creature's ever-changing presentiality. Again, as we saw, such presentiality bears upon divine knowledge and love that is especially relevant to human beings. The Father immediately and intimately knows, in his love that is the Holy Spirit, each human person in his Word/Son. Throughout the course of time, there is a personal relationship between the Trinity of persons and the human person, one in which the Father, in a timeless manner, knows in his Word and loves in his Spirit each human person.

1. *ST* I, 14, 13.

Now, within the covenantal acts of Jesus' death and resurrection, a new mixed relationship is established with the Trinity, one that *differs in kind* from that of the Creator/creature relationship. Because of this salvific relationship, there is a new presentiality. First, in his resurrection, Jesus, as the incarnate Son, is changed, and so he is *really* present to the Trinity in a new manner, and thus the Trinity is *actually* present to him, not because the Trinity has changed, but because there is a resurrected newness in Jesus. Second, those who abide in the risen Jesus, through the transforming sacraments of baptism and the Eucharist, are not simply *really* present *to* the Trinity but are *really* present *within* the Trinity. By abiding in the risen Jesus, the earthly time-bound faithful abide within the eternal Trinity and so share in their eternality. Because the members of Christ's body *really* abide in the Trinity, the persons of the Trinity are *actually* related to them in a new manner. That the persons of the Trinity do not change in *actually* being related to the faithful accentuates the fact that the faithful, as members of Christ's body, abide in the Trinity as the Trinity eternally and unchangeably exists.

Within this salvific presentiality, there is also a new manner of knowing and loving. Members of Christ's body now lovingly know, in the Holy Spirit, the Father to be their loving father—something they did not experientially know prior to abiding in Jesus, the Father's beloved Son. Likewise, the Father newly knows and loves those who abide in his risen incarnate Son, not because there is a change in him, but because of the new manner in which the faithful abide in Christ—within this new presentiality. Moreover, as the members of Christ's body here on earth continuously enact the contingent future within the flow of time—that is, their potentiality to grow in holiness—they are ever newly related, ever newly present, to the Trinity as the Trinity is.[2] The Father, then, ever knows the faithful through his Son and ever loves them in his Holy Spirit, not by way of a change in his divine knowing and loving, but by way of the changes within the faithful—their ever-new presentiality. Thus the persons of the Trinity ever possess, within this new presentialtiy, an immediate, intimate, and dynamic knowledge and love of the resurrected Christ and his body, as well as the whole of the created order, an order that is groaning as it awaits the bodily resurrection of the children of God. Likewise, what we perceive within this immediate, intimate, and dynamic knowledge and love between the Trinity and Christ and his members is the continuous deification of time. As the ever-maturing body of Christ grows in holiness over the course of time, so more and more does time assume the attributes that pertain to the Trinity's eternal manner of being—that of imperishable and immortal everlasting life.

Eschatological Presentiality

This deification of time obviously finds its completion when Jesus returns in glory at the end of time—time's new and everlasting eighth day. Having assumed the full likeness of Jesus, the risen Son, through the indwelling power of the Holy Spirit, the bodily risen members of his body obtain perfect communion with the Father as his children. In so becoming, earthly time ceases, for the new creation has found its completion in the risen Christ. Even though the saints in heaven and all of creation then embody the attributes

2. As noted above, sin, particularly mortal sin, can adversely affect this relationship. Also, I focus here exclusively on the members of Christ' body who are living on earth and so within time. Of course, the souls in purgatory, while being purified of the remnants of sin, are united to the Trinity in a manner that is conformable to their progressing state of holiness.

of divine eternity, because they remain bodily human, as well as creation retaining its materiality, the reality of duration remains—a foreverness that emulates and so replicates eternity. But this "heavenly duration," this heavenly presentiality, will not, it seems to me, contain within it the reality of time. This heavenly duration will be the ever-present and everlasting unchanging newness, the never growing old, that the saints will experience in sharing fully Jesus' filial vision of his Father in the love of the Holy Spirit—the seeing of the Father as he is.[3] As perfected adopted children of the Father, they become perfected images of the Father after the manner of his Son, for they perfectly abide in the risen Son. Thus they and the Father will wholly love one another in the Spirit. As the Trinity of persons *eternally* glory in their interrelated presence with and in one another, so members of Christ's body will *everlastingly* glory in their own interrelated presence with and in the persons of the Trinity—a new perichoretic oneness wherein earthly time is fully deified.[4]

The final question that arises is: Will the perfected saints, in communion with their risen Lord Jesus, enact acts as they everlast-

3. The persons of the Trinity do not experience "duration," for they are timelessly subsistent-relations-fully-in-act. Fully resurrected human beings, however, because they are bodily, will experience "duration"—their being ever glorified. Nonetheless, their experience of "duration" will not be timely in that they are ever present to the Trinity as the Trinity is, and so present in an unchanging manner—a manner that is timeless. Risen human beings will experience, unlike the Trinity, an ever-present "now," but a "now" that is timeless.

4. In the above, I am making a distinction between the "eternal" (timeless) glory that the Trinity experiences and the "everlasting" (durational though timeless) glory that human beings experience. Again, "eternality" contains no "now," but "everlasting-ness" does contain an enduring "now," though one that is ever timelessly new. The distinction being made is that the "non-divine" cannot be divine as the divine is divine. Thus, while human beings are incapable of being eternal as God is eternal, they can everlastingly share in his eternality in a manner appropriate to their being human.

ingly abide within their oneness in the Trinity? I would argue that the saints do enact acts, but they would not be acts wherein they would be changed, for such changes would entail the enacting of potential and so be marked by time. Rather, the acts that the saints enact in their risen bodily-ness would be acts performed within their now-unchanging perfection. They would be acts wherein the saints would express their perfect unchanging love for Jesus and the persons of the Trinity, as well as their perfect and unchanging love for one another—as perfected brothers and sisters in Christ. Moreover, the ministries and gifts, whether clerical or lay, that the saints enacted on earth would continue to be perfectly enacted in heaven, for the sake of the complete perfection of Christ's body. What the faithful did while on earth, which contributed to the building up of Christ's body, would find its perfected enactment within Christ's heavenly glorified body. Because of these perfectly enacted ministries and gifts, Christ's body would be perfected in its ever-new and everlasting completeness—"to mature manhood, of the measure of the stature of the fullness of Christ."[5] Here we perceive the ultimate importance of time. All the good that is timely enacted in Christ is the anticipation and furthering of time's full sanctification in eternity. Time finds its eschatological completeness in being subsumed into eternity.[6] In the above, I have attempted

---

5. Eph 4:13.

6. In this light, what is one to make of hell and those who will reside therein? At the coming of Jesus in glory at the end of time, those who are condemned will, like the just, rise bodily from the dead. But they obviously will not share in Jesus' perfect filial vision of the Father in the love of the Holy Spirit. Moreover, like the saints, the condemned will no longer exist in time, but they, also like the just, will experience an everlasting duration. The duration of the damned will be that of their everlasting condemnation. They too will enact acts, but the acts that they will perform will be those of anger and hatred toward Jesus and the blessed in heaven. They will forever blaspheme the Trinity. Their fury will never cease. I would also argue that the sins by which they condemned themselves to hell will rage within

to conceive properly and articulate correctly the relationship between the Trinity and Christ and his body, both as it pertains to the
temporal and heavenly order. I hope the intimacy and immediacy,
and so beauty, of this relationship has been made manifest.

---

them forever. The lustful, for example, will burn with passion forever, an obsession
addiction that will never be satisfied, and so they will never find sexual fulfillment,
but rather they will experience the rage of unfulfilled desire. The greedy will forever, in frenzied craving, desire wealth and power only to be eternally infuriated that
their selfish fixation will never be achieved. Hell will be hell for the condemned,
for what they passionately desired on earth will forever mockingly be unfulfilled in
hell. Sinful time finds it eschatological fulfillment in the foreverness of hell.

Conclusion

I do not think much needs to be said by way of conclusion. I would simply like to highlight four points.

First, as I noted in the introduction, one of the original contributions found in this study is the placing of the eternity and time within the context of the Trinity and not simply in relation to the one God. In doing so, I have rendered a more accurate examination since God *is* a Trinity of persons. Moreover, at the heart of this entire study is my emphasis concerning the various relationships that exist between the eternal Trinity and time—both within the act of creation and within acts of salvation. In Part I, I emphasized that the divine act of creation established a *mixed relationship*, one wherein creation, and particularly human beings, are *really* related to the Trinity in that they come to exist. Because creation and human beings are *really* related to the persons of the Trinity as they exist in themselves, the Trinity is *actually* related to creation and humankind in an immediate, intimate, and unbreakable manner. Thus, within the Trinity's eternality, the divine persons love and know all that is. As creation and human persons enact their potential throughout time, they are ever newly related to the Trinity, and so the persons of the Trinity are ever related to them as they presently exist, in their presentiality, within the flow of time. Thus the persons of the Trinity love and know creation and humankind not by way of a change within their eternal unchanging nature, but by way of the timely changes that inhere within creation and human beings. Within the contingencies of time, the Trinity is ever present to, in its eternal and unchanging love and knowledge, the enacted contingency.

Second, the mixed relationship between the Trinity and creation, between eternity and time, established by the act of creation, is the foundational relationship upon which the new salvific relationship comes to be. In Part II, we saw that this new salvific relationship differs in kind from that of the Creator/creation relationship, for it does not simply unite eternity and time but subsumes time into eternity—into the eternal life of the Trinity. Through the act of the Incarnation, the eternal Son of God comes to exist as man in time. Eternity and time find their unity in Jesus. As man, the Son of God, through his saving death, resurrection, and subsequent pouring out of the Holy Spirit, has made it possible for humankind, and all of creation, to abide within the Trinity itself. Through baptism, those who believe become living, Spirit-transformed, members of Christ's body, and so become children of the heavenly Father. This new intimacy finds its earthly summit within the Eucharist. Christians become one in the risen Jesus as the risen Jesus truly is, and so they abide in one another. Thus, in Christ, time is taken up into eternity. Moreover, we saw that this new relationship between the risen Christ and his body is a *real* relationship, for both Christ and the members of his body are changed over the course of time. As new members enter into the body of Christ and as the body of Christ grows in holiness, time is ever divinized—it being evermore subsumed into the risen reality of the risen Jesus. The faithful, already in time, assume the divine attributes of imperishability and immortality.

Third, the *real* relationship between Jesus and his body in turn establishes a new relationship with the persons of the Trinity. This relationship is again *mixed*. Although the persons of the Trinity are not changed in this relationship, they are *actually* related to the risen Jesus and so to his body, because the risen Jesus and his body are *really* related to the Trinity. Thus the persons of the Trinity, within their eternal unchanging being, love and know Christ and his body as it changes and matures over the course of time—in time's ever-changing presentiality. This salvific relationship finds its conclusion, as we saw, when Jesus returns in glory at the end of time, and humankind and the whole of creation are fully subsumed into Christ and so abide within the eternal life of the Trinity itself. Thus, as time began in the act of creation, so it finds its completion in the last act of re-creation—the making of all things newly one in Christ. The Trinity, then, called time into being that it might share everlastingly in its eternity. Lastly, while I hope that I have provided some clarity to the various mysteries involved concerning the eternal Trinity and its relationship to created time, what is evident is that such mysteries cannot be fully comprehended. We may know more clearly what the mysteries are, yet we are incapable of fully grasping the entirety of their inherent meaning. The point of this philosophical and theological enterprise was not, then, to obtain comprehension, but to glory in the mysteries themselves—in their very incomprehensibility. To contemplate the beauty of these mysteries in time is but the prelude to forever contemplating their awesomeness in eternity.

WORKS CONSULTED

Aquinas, Thomas. *De Ente et Essentia*. Translation from Armand Maurer, trans., *On Being and Essence*. Toronto: Pontifical Institute of Mediaeval Studies, 1968.

———. *Summa Theologica*. Translated by the Fathers of the English Dominican Province. New York: Benziger Brothers, 1946.

Bankston, Will. "Seeing God's Essence: A Teleological Coordination of the Beatific Vision and Christ's Work of Atonement." *Pro Ecclesia* 30, no. 4 (2021): 539–66.

Beilby, James, K., and Paul, R. Eddy, eds. *Divine Foreknowledge: Four Views*. Downers Grove, IL: InterVarsity, 2001.

Bonaventure. *Disputed Questions on the Mystery of the Trinity*. In *Works of Saint Bonaventure*, vol. 3. St. Bonaventure, NY: Franciscan Institute, 1979.

Bradshaw, David. "Time and Eternity in the Greek Fathers." *The Thomist* 70 (2006): 311–66.

Braine, David. *The Reality of Time and the Existence of God*. Oxford: Clarendon Press, 1988.

Brent, James. "God's Knowledge and Will." In *The Oxford Handbook on Aquinas*, edited by Brian Davies and Eleonore Stump, 158–71. Oxford: Oxford University Press, 2012.

Burrell, David. *Aquinas: God and Action*. London: Routledge & Kegan Paul, 1979.

———. "Divine Eternity." *Faith and Philosophy: Journal of the Society of Christian Philosophers* 1, no. 4 (1984): 389–406.

———. "God's Knowledge of Future Contingents: A Reply to William Lane Craig." *The Thomist* 58, no. 2 (1994): 317–22.

Craig, William Lane. "Divine Eternity." In *The Oxford Handbook of Philosophical Theology*, edited by Thomas P. Flint and Michael C. Rea, 145–66. Oxford: Oxford University Press, 2009.

Dodds, Michael. *The Unchanging God of Love: Thomas Aquinas and Contemporary Theology on Divine Immutability*. Washington, DC: Catholic University of America Press, 2008.

———. *The One Creator God in Thomas Aquinas and Contemporary Theology*. Washington, DC: Catholic University of America Press, 2020.

Dolezal, E. James. "Defending Divine Impassibility." In *Classical Theism: New Essays on the Metaphysics of God*, edited by Robert C. Koons and Jonathan Fuqua. London: Routledge, forthcoming.

Durand, Emmanuel. "A Theology of God the Father." In *The Oxford Handbook of the Trinity*, edited by Gilles Emery and Matthew Levering, 371–86. Oxford: Oxford University Press, 2011.

———. "The Trinity." In *The Oxford Handbook of Catholic Theology*, edited by Lewis Ayers and Medi Ann Volpe, 151–66. Oxford: Oxford University Press, 2019.

Emery, Gilles. *Trinity in Aquinas*. Ave Maria, FL: Sapientia Press, 2003.

Ganssle, Gregory, E., ed. *God and Time: Four Views*. Downers Grove, IL: InterVarsity Press, 2001.

Garrigou-Lagrange, Reginald. *The One God: A Commentary on the First Part of St. Thomas' Theological Summa*. St. Louis: Herder, 1943.

Geach, Peter. "Omniscience and the Future." In *Providence and Evil*, 40–66. Cambridge: Cambridge University Press, 1997.

Goris, Harm, J. M. J. *Free Creatures of an Eternal God: Thomas Aquinas on God's Infallible Foreknowledge and Irresistible Will*. Nijmegen: Thomistic Institute of Etrecht, 1996.

Henninger, M. *Relations: Medieval Theories, 1250–1325*. Oxford: Clarendon Press, 1989.

Hill, William. "Does God Know the Future? Aquinas and Some Moderns." *Theological Studies* 36 (1975): 3–18.

Kim, Eunsoo. *Time, Eternity, and the Trinity: A Trinitarian Analogical Understanding of Time and Eternity*. Eugene, OR: Pickwick Publications, 2010.

Krempel, Anton. *La Doctrine de la Relation chez Saint Thomas*. Paris: J. Vrin, 1952.

Kretzmann, Norman. "Omniscience and Immutability." *Journal of Philosophy* 63 (1966): 408–21.

Leftow, Brian. "God's Impassibility, Immutability, and Eternality." In *The Oxford Handbook of Aquinas*, edited by Brian Davies and Eleonore Stump, 173–86. Oxford: Oxford University Press, 2012.

Mann, William E. "Simplicity and Immutability of God." In *The Concept of God*, edited by Thomas V. Morris, 253–67. Oxford: Oxford University Press, 1987.

Muller, Earl. "Real Relations and the Divine: Issues in Thomas's Understanding of God's Relation to the Word." *Theological Studies* 56 (1995): 673–95.

Neville, Robert. *God the Creator: On the Transcendence and Presence of God*. Chicago: University of Chicago Press, 1968.

Ormerod, Neal. "'And We Shall See Him Face to Face': A Trinitarian Analysis of the Beatific Vision." *Theological Studies* 82, no. 4 (2021): 646–62.

Ormerod Neal, and Jacobs-Vandegeer Christiaan. "Sacred Heart, Beatific Mind: Exploring the Consciousness of Jesus." *Theological Studies* 79, no. 4 (2018): 727–44.

Piolata, Thomas. "*Unitas caritatis*: A Reading of Bonaventure's *Quaestiones disputatae de mysterio Trinitatis* (with a Focus on the Spirit)." STL thesis, Pontifical Gregorian University, 2021.

Scheeben, Matthias Joseph. *The Mysteries of Christianity*. St. Louis: B. Herder, 1946.

———. *Handbook of Catholic Dogmatics, Book Two: Doctrine about God or Theology in the Narrative Sense*. Steubenville, OH: Emmaus Academic, 2021.

Shanley, Brian. "Eternal Knowledge of the Temporal in Aquinas." *American Catholic Philosophical Quarterly* 71, no. 2 (1997): 197–224.

———. "Aquinas on God's Causal Knowledge: A Reply to Stump and Kretzmann." *American Catholic Philosophical Quarterly* 72, no. 3 (1998): 447–57.

Stump, Eleonore. *Aquinas*. New York: Routledge, 2003.

————. "Divine Simplicity." In *The Oxford Handbook of Aquinas*, edited by Brian Davies and Eleonore Stump, 135–46. Oxford: Oxford University Press, 2012.

————. *The God of the Bible and the God of the Philosophers*. Milwaukee: Marquette University Press, 2016.

Stump, Eleonore, and Norman Kretzmann. "Absolute Simplicity." *Faith and Philosophy: Journal of the Society of Christian Philosophers* 2, no. 4 (1985): 353–82.

————. "Eternity." In *The Concept of God*, edited by Thomas V. Morris, 219–52. Oxford: Oxford University Press, 1987.

————. "Eternity, Awareness, and Action." *Faith and Philosophy: Journal of the Society of Christian Philosophers* 9, no. 4 (1992): 463–82.

————. "Eternity and God's Knowledge: A Reply to Shanley." *American Catholic Philosophical Quarterly* 72, no. 3 (1998): 439–45.

Sturch, Richard. "Divine Knowledge: Comparisons and Contrasts with Human Knowledge." *Tyndale Bulletin* 47, no. 1 (1996): 123–42.

Ward, Keith. "The Temporality of God." *International Journal for Philosophy and Religion* 50 (2001): 253–69.

Weinandy, Thomas G. *Does God Change? The Word's Becoming in the Incarnation*. Still River, MA: St. Bede's, 1985.

Weinandy, Thomas G. *Does God Suffer?* Edinburgh: T&T Clark, 2000.

————. "Aquinas: God *IS* Man—The Marvel of the Incarnation." In *Aquinas on Doctrine: A Critical Introduction*, edited by Thomas G. Weinandy, Daniel A. Keating, and John P. Yocum, 67–89 London: T&T Clark, 2004.

————. "Trinitarian Christology: The Eternal Son." In *The Oxford Handbook of the Trinity*, edited by Gilles Emery and Matthew Levering, 387–99. Oxford: Oxford University Press, 2011.

————. "Jesus' Filial Vision of the Father." In *Jesus: Essays in Christology*, 279–92. Ave Maria, FL: Sapientia Press, 2014.

————. "Thomas Joseph White's Beatific Vision of the Incarnate Son: A Response." In *Jesus: Essays in Christology*, 293–301. Ave Maria, FL: Sapientia Press, 2014.

————. "The Doctrinal Significance of the Councils of Nicaea, Ephesus, and Chalcedon." In *The Oxford Handbook of Christology*, edited by Francesca Aran Murphy, 549–67. Oxford: Oxford University Press, 2015.

———. *Jesus the Christ*. Huntington, IN: Our Sunday Visitor Press, 2003. Repr., Ex Fontibus Press, 2017.

———. *Jesus Becoming Jesus: A Theological Interpretation of the Synoptic Gospels*. Washington, DC: Catholic University of America Press, 2018.

———. "Paul's Conversion in His Own Words." In *The Book of Acts: Catholic, Orthodox, and Evangelical Readings*, edited by Charles Raith II, 175–87. Washington, DC: Catholic University of America Press, 2019.

———. "The Incarnation." In *The Oxford Handbook of Catholic Theology*, edited by Lewis Ayers and Medi Ann Volpe, 167–82. Oxford: Oxford University Press, 2019.

———. "The Trinity's Loving Act of Creation." In *The Oxford Handbook of Catholic Theology*, edited by Lewis Ayers and Medi Ann Volpe, 124–38. Oxford: Oxford University Press, 2019.

———. *Jesus Becoming Jesus: A Theological Interpretation of the Gospel of John: Prologue and the Book of Signs*, vol. 2. Washington, DC: Catholic University of America Press, 2021.

———. "The Trinity: The Father's Spirit of Sonship—Further Considerations on Reconceiving the Trinity." In *Engaging Catholic Doctrine: Essays in Honor of Matthew Levering*, edited by Robert Barron, Scott W. Hahn, and James R. A. Merrick. Steubenville, OH: Emmaus Academic, forthcoming.

White, Thomas Joseph. "Divine Simplicity and the Holy Trinity." *International Journal of Systematic Theology* 18, no. 1 (2016): 66–93.

———. "Nicene Orthodoxy and Trinitarian Simplicity." *American Catholic Philosophical Quarterly* 90, no. 4 (2016): 727–50.

Wright, John. "Divine Knowledge and Human Freedom: The God Who Dialogues." *Theological Studies* 38 (1977): 450–77.

The Trinity: Eternity and Time was designed in Minion and composed by Kachergis Book Design of Pittsboro, North Carolina. It was printed on 60-pound House Natural Smooth and bound by Sheridan Books of Chelsea, Michigan.